You'll Laugh, You'll Weep, You'll Never Forget!

No fiction writer could get away with the torrent of astonishing, unexpected events in this book. You'll laugh, you'll weep, you'll never forget.

Ralph D. Winter
Founder, U.S. Center for World Missions

Paul Eshleman's book challenges each of us to believe God for the impossible!

Josh McDowell
Josh McDowell Ministries

This dramatic and authentic book will bring great joy and praise to those who read it. I joyfully recommend it.

Paul A. Cedar
Chairman, Lausanne Committee for
World Evangelization

This book should have the word "miracle" stamped on the cover. My belief is that the incredible stories Paul Eshleman shares are only a fraction of all God is doing through The JESUS Film Project.

David R. Mains
Chapel Ministries, Inc.

If you've longed to see the hand of God at work in unique and supernatural ways, then read this account of God's strategic empowerment of the "JESUS" film. Your life will be enriched.

Joe Stowell
President, Moody Bible Institute

The Touch of Jesus recounts one of the great stories of global evangelism in the history of the Church. Paul Eshleman's illustrations of the global impact of the "JESUS" film truly ought to be added to any list of "signs and wonders" that the Church is presently seeing in its greatest-ever hour of harvest.

Dick Eastman
International President, Every Home for Christ

The Touch of Jesus reads like the Book of Acts. It will stir your soul.

Dr. Paul A. Kienel
President Emeritus, Association of Christian
Schools International

I highly recommend this exciting account of how millions around the world have been converted through viewing the "JESUS" film.

Vinson Synan
Dean, Regent University School of Divinity

The Touch of Jesus presents dynamic evidence of how God is using the "JESUS" film to bring literally millions of people to Christ.

Floyd McClung
Metro Christian Fellowship, Kansas City, MO

The Touch of Jesus dramatically tells the story of the life-transforming power of Jesus in the lives of individuals, cities, and nations touched by Jesus through the "JESUS" film. If you read this book, you will receive a fresh touch of Jesus.

Luis Bush
International Mission Leader,
AD 2000 & Beyond Movement

Whether in closed countries, illiterate cultures, or in places of open harvest, the graphic portrayal of the gospel in the "JESUS" film has radically accelerated the potential for fulfilling the Great Commission. This book will make you sense that you are reading a sequel to the Book of Acts.

Jerry Rankin
President,
Southern Baptist International Mission Board

"JESUS" film team members have only one purpose as expressed in this beautiful book: "To make sure that there are no boys or girls, men or women who don't get at least one chance to hear about Jesus." *The Touch of Jesus* tells us a lot about what the committed film team members are doing to fulfill this purpose, and also says something important about what we must do and how to do it: for love alone!

Fr. Tom Forrest, C.Ss.R.
Washington, D.C.

THE TOUCH OF JESUS

PAUL ESHLEMAN

*New**Life***
PUBLICATIONS
A MINISTRY OF CAMPUS CRUSADE FOR CHRIST

The Touch of Jesus

Published by
NewLife Publications
A ministry of Campus Crusade for Christ
100 Lake Hart Drive
Orlando, FL 32832

Design and typesetting by Genesis Publications.

Printed in the United States of America.

Library of Congress Cataloging-in-Publication Data
Eshleman, Paul.
    The touch of Jesus / Paul Eshleman.
        p. cm.
    Includes bibliographical references.
    ISBN 1-56399-071-7 — ISBN 1-56399-067-9 (hardcover)
    1. Motion pictures in missionary work. 2. Jesus (Motion picture)
3. Missions—History—20th century.   I. Title.
BV2082.A8E84   1995
266'.009'049—dc20   95-4462
                                                     CIP

Unless otherwise noted, Scripture quotations are from the *New International Version,* ©1973, 1978, 1984 by the International Bible Society. Published by Zondervan Bible Publishers, Grand Rapids, Michigan.

Scripture quotations designated NASB are from the *New American Standard Bible,* © 1960, 1962, 1963, 1968, 1971, 1972, 1975, 1977 by the Lockman Foundation, La Habra, California.

NewLife2000 is a registered trademark of Campus Crusade for Christ Inc.

To the courageous film team workers whose tireless dedication has taken Jesus to the corners of the earth.

Contents

Acknowledgments

This book has been a team effort involving Don Tanner, Jean Bryant, Joette Whims, Lynn Copeland, Helen Hoeksema, and Donna Bahler. I want to express my grateful appreciation for their faithful labors in research and editing, helping me articulate the thrilling accounts of sacrifice and commitment by the "JESUS" film teams who are reaching millions who have never heard of Jesus. I am also grateful for the valued comments of those who have given their endorsements of this book.

Foreword

No matter where in the world I run into Paul Eshleman, I always ask, "Please, do you have a few moments to tell me a 'JESUS' film story?" The last time I saw him, he smiled, rubbed his chin, and replied, "Well, our team just got back from Mongolia, and you'll never believe what happened there..."

For the next few minutes, I always sit enthralled, listening to stories of modern-day missionaries taking the "JESUS" film to nations around the globe—hacking their way through thick jungles; over prison walls; down dusty, rutted roads; climbing treacherous mountains; and tiptoeing through dangerous political hot spots—all to show the love of Christ to a lost world.

Just listening to Paul describe how God is using the film to reach people from Mongolia to Mozambique pumps my heart. My mind is expanded, and my horizons are stretched. And my vision is always refreshed after hearing these marvelous testimonies; I'm reenergized to go out and touch for Christ those needy and searching people whom God has placed in my own sphere of life.

The "JESUS" film continues to cause powerful repercussions around the globe. Hundreds of thousands of people are coming to Christ as a result of the many teams who take this film into unreached areas; but also, the film is shaking up the rest of us on the homefront who are emblazoned and emboldened to proclaim Christ in our own communities. This is what happens when you hear the powerful testimonies of God's redemptive grace.

And it's what happens to me every time I hear how God is using the "JESUS" film. Thankfully, now I don't have to wait to run into Paul Eshleman to hear his modern-day missions stories from the field. Paul finally has done what many of us have been asking him to do for years: "Write it down."

That's why I'm so grateful that you are holding *The Touch of Jesus* in your hands. I'm convinced that you, too, will gain a fresh zeal for fulfilling the Great Commission as you travel with the

11

"JESUS" teams in this book to the uttermost corners of the earth. You will meet a KGB agent. You will encounter a young African girl who watched her mother be mauled by a lion. You will learn about a Muslim nomad who lives on the edges of an African desert. And you will see all of these, and many more, lay all on the altar for Christ.

And who knows? After hearing what God has done in their lives, you may end up feeling the touch of Jesus in your own life as well. And when you do, wild horses won't be able to stop you from giving His touch to lost and hurting people in your own world.

Joni Eareckson Tada
President, JAF Ministries

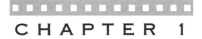

CHAPTER 1

When Heaven Came Down

I t was nearing dark when the lion attacked. For days the small family, weakened by starvation and disease, had struggled through the South African bush. The 16-year-old girl's father was dead, and her brave little mother was taking the children on one last march to find food.

Refugees from Mozambique, they needed to cross the forty-mile-wide game reserve on the border of the Republic of South Africa.

Conditions in Mozambique were desperate. Since gaining independence from Portugal more than fifteen years ago, this family's country had been wracked by civil war. The rebel group Renamo was fighting everywhere, and atrocities committed by both the Marxist government and Renamo were commonplace. Missionaries had been killed, women raped, schools burned, and bands of outlaws had stolen the last remaining possessions from the survivors.

The Marxist government was in shambles. Nothing worked. The ports sat empty. No ships arrived because no one had money to buy their goods. The shelves of the stores were bare, and the entire country was grappling with the throes of death.

Five hundred thousand refugees crowded camps in nearby countries, begging for food. For a price, a guide would take them across the dangerous game reserve filled with lions. The trek cannot be made in one day, so he would take refugees to the big trees that could be climbed, and they would be safe for the night. But the hungry, desperate mother had no money for a guide, so she had set out alone.

13

They had struggled along for some time in the deepening dusk when suddenly a lion burst from his cover and knocked the mother to the ground. In panic, the daughter grabbed the baby off her mother's back, took the four-year-old by the hand and ran. The screams of her mother filled her ears as she stumbled through the deep brush.

She looked back and saw to her horror that the lion was eating her mother. But she could do nothing. She must take the children and escape.

Tears streamed down her cheeks and her heart was breaking inside, but she kept going. Just a few more miles perhaps. She didn't know. Lungs bursting. Baby hungry. Little sister crying. Mother dead. Run. Run. Run.

And finally—she made it!

She saw smoking fires of a refugee camp in the distance. On spindly legs, in tattered clothes and exhausted, she gathered her little sister into her arms and panted, "It'll be all right. We'll be safe and we'll find food. Everything will be all right when we get to that place."

But when they arrived at "that place," they found a cesspool of human misery, peopled by walking skeletons who stared through vacant eyes at the new arrivals. It was a place without hope ...

I learned of this tragic incident, of the camp, and more, from Marie Erasmus who, with her husband, Willie, had been there.

Places without hope were those to which I was personally challenged to go. People without hope were those to whom we wanted to take the "JESUS" film, with His message of love and forgiveness—and hope.

This camp was one of those places, and these refugees were some of those people. Marie and Willie would go to them, and in the process Marie and Willie would be changed forever themselves.

This couple directed the translation and distribution of the "JESUS" film across South Africa, as well as showings of the film with a team. They had completed their seventh language translation of "JESUS," this one in the "click-click" bushman language featured in the Hollywood film, "The Gods Must Be Crazy." "JESUS" was the first film to be translated in its entirety into this unusual language.

This was Giyani, Gazankulu, in South Africa, and Marie and Willie came to show the "JESUS" film in one of the refugee camps. The pretty, blond Afrikaaner with her compassionate heart for blacks in South Africa belied the stereotype of white South Africans so favored by Western media.

Shimmering waves of heat rose in the distance as the blazing African sun beat down on the film team truck. The vehicle's passing interrupted only briefly the stillness of the African bush and soon all was quiet again. Gritty red dust hung in the air, the only evidence of recent movement.

As she and Willie drove into the refugee camp, Marie said with pain, "Just look at these people. They have nothing."

She was the one who had recounted to me the story of the girl who escaped from the lion's attack. She wondered how many sitting around the smoking fires could tell similar stories of horror and loss. How much bloodshed had they seen? How many husbands, fathers, wives, mothers, children had been lost in senseless slaughter and starvation?

Willie maneuvered the van along the makeshift roads through the camp, looking for the best open place to show the film. But the hovels were everywhere.

Willie and Marie Erasmus, African film pioneers

"It's hard to believe anyone can actually live in these places," Marie told me later. "They live in mud huts, or 'homes' made of cardboard boxes or crates. Some have filled beer cans with sand in an attempt to build a wall. Others slap mud over sticks and brush to make a shelter into which they can crawl at night."

They had no water and little food. One meal a day from the meager relief rations barely staved off the slow agony of starvation. The fetid, striking odor of human excrement gagged the senses. And always the blank, staring eyes—beyond feeling. A dress given here or a blouse given there yielded no comment. What good is a dress when your baby is dying of malnutrition or diarrhea, and your husband is gone?

Willie finally found a spot, and through the hot afternoon he, Marie, and the team began preparing for the showing.

On an earlier trip to the area, a young missionary had met them as they finished distributing clothing. "Please bring your film to the camp where I work," he had begged.

"We haven't yet translated it into the Shangaan language that these people speak," Willie protested.

"It's okay. We'll interpret it while it is being shown."

Since he had worked in the camp, the young missionary had gathered about forty people who had become believers in Christ, and they started a church. The new Christians had been taught to share their faith in Christ and were prepared to counsel interested people after the film showing.

As the team set up the free-standing two-sided movie screen, the people's curiosity began to build. Children swarmed around the team jabbering excitedly while some of the older ones watched in wonder.

But something was wrong.

Marie sensed demonic oppression building. Then the team heard witch doctors chanting and saw them throwing bones on the ground in satanic rituals. With howling and incantations, the witch doctors began calling up spirits of their ancestors. An eerie and foreboding pall seemed to fall over the camp.

Willie called the team together to pray.

Thirty other trainers and trainees had come from the nearby New Life Training Center to participate in this evangelistic outreach. Half of their instruction was to be in the field. This film showing would be an excellent opportunity to put into practice what they had learned in the classroom.

However, this would not be just the usual practical experience in evangelism. This was spiritual warfare.

They all began to pray. For three hours they implored God to send His blessings, bind the power of the evil one, and open the eyes of the spiritually blind. As they finished their prayers together, they joined hands and walked around in a circle, symbolically encircling the camp. They asked God to tear down the spiritual walls as He had destroyed the walls of Jericho. As darkness set in, the ragged refugees came out of their shacks and began to stream toward the showing area.

The witch doctors stopped their dancing. More people arrived. Perhaps the children who escaped from the lions were in the audience. It was hard to tell.

As with most showings in Africa, the children sat in the dust and as close as possible to the screen. Ropes stretched between the projector and the sides of the screen established a little open space in front of the projector that could eventually be used for counseling. In the meantime, it would keep hands and heads out of the picture.

Behind the children were the mothers with babies. Some of the babies showed swollen bellies, the first evidence of *kwashiorkor*, the dreaded disease of malnutrition that claims so many in their first year.

And as the darkness deepened and the film was started, the men of the tribe filled in around the edges in the back.

A "JESUS" film showing is a cultural event that draws the entire village.

The interpreter stood with a microphone beside the projector. The English soundtrack was turned to a low level. Line by line he translated what was taking place on the screen.

Finding an empty space between the huts had been difficult. Now there were more than a thousand people crowded into a small dusty clearing.

Between reels, the interpreter explained the significance of what they were seeing. He told why it was important that Mary be a virgin and how only a supernatural man could be God.

"During the scenes of the crucifixion in the fourth 30-minute reel," Marie said, "we sensed something unusual happening. Everyone began to cry—the women *and* the men—a mournful wailing that gradually rose from the crowd in a relentless crescendo.

"At almost all film showings a few people cry," she observed, "but this was different. When the film showed Jesus being pushed down the Via Dolorosa, the weeping became louder and uncontrollable. When the Roman soldiers started nailing Jesus to the cross, many of the people jumped up and ran toward the screen with their hands in the air and crying out to God.

"They ignored all the ropes, and huge clouds of dust filled the air as people watching from both sides of the screen rushed to the front."

Rivers of tears poured down dirty cheeks. Young men, old men, and women beat their breasts and cried out, "Oh, God! Oh, God!" Some were on their knees, some stood with eyes closed and arms raised, others lay prostrate on the ground. The interpreter lay on his back in the dirt, praying, thanking God, crying, praising, worshipping, confessing. Everywhere people were confessing their sins. The film was forgotten. These people were in the presence of a holy God, and they were overwhelmed.

Someone turned the projector off. The film team rushed to pray with and counsel those who were seeking God. But they couldn't speak. One by one, the team members themselves fell to their knees, confessing their own sins.

"I can't explain how I felt," Willie told me later. "I felt the awesome power of God. I felt His love, His compassion, His care. It was overpowering. It was a wave that welled up inside us and we couldn't contain it. We were totally, irrevocably, hopelessly in love with Jesus. And the experience just burst out of us with confession and tears, and praise, and worship, and a feeling of wonder."

Tears came to his eyes. "I saw a nine-year-old boy crying out to God. I turned to pray for him, but I couldn't because I was crying myself. A seventy-year-old man with his eyes open and his hands in the air, repeated over and over again, 'I just saw Jesus! I just saw Jesus!' But we were not just seeing the portrayal of Jesus; we were feeling His presence so powerfully that we just couldn't take it in."

Marie's experience was the same. "When the Holy Spirit began to move across the crowd, I went over to some of the women to pray with them. All around me, women were on their knees, eyes closed, hands lifted, crying out to God.

"I started to pray with one woman, but I couldn't speak. I was overcome—confessing my own sins. The sense of God's presence, His power and holiness, was so great that no one could do anything but confess sin. I knew I was in a holy, holy place."

It was hard for Marie to speak as she recalled these deep, personal moments with God. "The feeling I got was that God's love is just so big that if He gives you even a little touch of it, you simply can't contain it. I never experienced anything like it in my whole life. These people had nothing. And God decided to give to them—right there in that filthy camp—a chance to feel His presence and His love."

When they had driven into the camp, Marie and Willie and their team went first to the church, and they heard singing: "God is so good, God is so good." The team had printed the word *counselor* on paper plates and pinned them to the shirts of the newly trained Christians. But when all of this started to take place, those counselors were soon on their knees along with the film team—bowing before their loving, holy God.

More than thirty minutes passed. Still the sounds of weeping and passionate prayer filled the field.

Willie went to the interpreter. "We need to finish the film so they will know the good news of the resurrection." The interpreter resumed his place by the projector and the film began again. All across the audience people continued to wipe tears from their eyes.

They saw the burial of Christ, and then—the resurrection. The interpreter explained to the crowd, "Jesus died to make the payment for our sins. But death could not hold Him." And with that, he pointed to the screen and shouted with uncontainable joy, "And there He is! He was raised from the dead!"

The crowd exploded as if a dam had burst. Everyone began cheering and dancing and hugging one another and jumping up and down.

The team never finished showing the film. An invitation was given for all of those who wanted to receive Christ to come to the front. The "problem" was, they *all* wanted to accept Him as their Savior and Lord—all one thousand.

Individual counseling was impossible, so they all were counseled at one time. After the counseling ended, the team and the counselors returned to their circles and sang and danced and shared and prayed, praising God for what He had done. Revival had come to them. They would never be the same.

The following Sunday, five hundred new believers showed up trying to get into the forty-person church. They started immediately to build a larger hut to contain the spiritual harvest.

Marie marveled at what God had done. "God is so great," she told me. "These people had nothing. They felt absolutely hopeless. They desperately needed to belong to someone, to feel loved.

This scene shows Jesus during His crucifixion.

That night *heaven came down* and God brought to their impoverished hearts His indescribable love. Everyone, even the counselors and the entire film team, experienced an almost unbelievable supernatural event—the life-changing, heart-rending touch of Jesus!"

What a night! It was just one experience, in just one camp, with just one "JESUS" film team. But those kinds of events have been occurring all over the world. As you read the following chapters and realize the widespread and seemingly incredible influence of our wonderful, loving God, I pray that your own faith will be deepened and broadened, and that you will be challenged to find new ways to express that faith.

The Holy Spirit descends like a dove on Jesus after His baptism in the Jordan River.

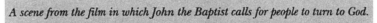

A scene from the film in which John the Baptist calls for people to turn to God.

Jesus feeds the 5,000 with five loaves and two fish.

The miracle of the huge catch of fish.

CHAPTER 2

Behind the Iron Curtain

T he touch of Jesus," Marie had said.

I thought of how desperately the people of the Iron Curtain countries also needed to feel that supernatural touch, the touch that could not only heal physically, but also could reach down into a discouraged, defeated heart and give real hope. Hope for this life on earth; but more importantly, a hope for an eternal, unending life with the Creator in heaven.

By 1988, we still had made no progress in getting the "JESUS" film into the Soviet Union. Every effort had been met by the Communists with utter disdain and complete rejection.

One day, as I walked out of an Intourist Hotel in Estonia, I noticed a KGB agent following me. He carried a black leather tote bag and was dressed in Western clothes. I passed him; then I turned back suddenly and caught him staring at me. The top of his bag was open. True tourists are usually more careful to keep their bags zipped up lest something fall out or get stolen. KGB agents carry walkie-talkies and need to have them handy without being visible.

I didn't have time to check out his shoes. That was usually a dead giveaway. Western tourists didn't wear the thick-soled, out-of-style shoes made in the Soviet Union that somewhat resembled retreaded truck tires.

So, I thought, *they are following us.* But it really didn't matter; we were just going to church.

It was a church that had been registered with the government, and it was packed. People walking by could hear the speaking, would come in, and stand all across the back. I was to give a report on how God was using the "JESUS" film in Nepal, Indonesia, and other parts of Asia.

About two-thirds of the way through my talk, two men in the balcony got up and walked out. Our KGB watchers. I wondered what I had said. I could remember nothing inflammatory or controversial, so I presumed it was just time for them to check in with their bosses.

Since I was speaking in back-to-back church services, my companion and I had to leave before the first one wrapped up. As we walked out, we noticed one of our "friends" in line at the soda pop machine. We arranged ourselves so we could wait for our ride to the next church and also observe him watching us. We were facing him, so he had a tough time looking at us without being obvious. He didn't do too well. When he finally got up to the pop machine, he didn't know what to do so he went back to the end of the line. And every time he glanced back to see if we were still there, we were looking right at him.

Nobody followed as we drove to the next church. We wondered why. When we returned to our hotel later that night, a new television had been placed in our room. No doubt the KGB had done a full search of all of our suitcases and papers. Apparently, we had been followed just so they could be sure we wouldn't come back while they were doing their search. Also, if somehow their men should lose us and we found the others in our room, they could say they were just bringing in the new TV.

Of course, as always, our room was bugged. Although they probably are capable of listening in on every room, some floors get special attention. In one city I was given the same hotel and the same room that Billy Graham, Bill Bright, and several other Christian leaders had been assigned when they visited there.

One night we tried for twenty minutes to get our TV to work. We could get the sound, but no picture. I said, "It's all the listening equipment in the TV that messes up the picture." Within five seconds, the picture came on.

One day we rode up in the elevator with two of the agents. It was hot in the city; the hotels were not air-conditioned, and in the sweltering 100-degree weather everyone was struggling to stay cool. In fact, it was so hot that the KGB left open the door to their "listening room" on our floor. The room was two doors down from us.

They stepped into the room and put on their earphones. We continued down to our own room and discussed what we should say to them.

We decided to read the Scriptures to them. I turned my head up a little toward the fire sprinkler on the ceiling in case the microphone was there.

"We'd just like to say 'hello' to you men there in the listening room," I began. "I don't know if you have a Bible, but if you do, we will be reading today from the book of Psalms, which is right in the middle of the Bible."

Several weeks before, I had gone through Psalms and underlined every verse that contained the word *praise.* For the next hour we read those passages to them. I don't know whether they continued to listen, but we were wonderfully blessed. As we read those verses aloud, our own faith was strengthened by the fact that one day these tense, closed conditions would be lifted, and we believed we would proclaim the message of Christ openly. I thought of that great praise song:

There is strength in the name of the Lord.
There is power in the name of the Lord.
There is hope in the name of the Lord.
Blessed is he who comes in the name of the Lord. [1]

We were coming in the name of Jesus, the one who saves, keeps, and delivers—eternally.

We had been working with Christians in the Soviet Union, but meeting our contacts was never easy. We had to change buses, get in and out of taxicabs, walk through parks, and arrange meetings on particular park benches. Even for the most committed pastors and Christian workers, life was extremely difficult.

I met pastors who were afraid to have telephones. They didn't want to be called by people from the West who might not be sensitive to their security problems.

Decades of persecution for personal witnessing had dulled aggressive outreaches. Constant harassment and intimidation by officials had left many pastors fearful of doing anything new.

---

[1] "In the Name of the Lord" by Sandi Patti Helvering/Gloria Gaither/Phil McHugh © 1986 by Sandi's Songs Music (adm. by Addison Music Co.)/ Gaither Music Co. (adm. by Gaither Copyright Management)/River Oaks Music Co. (adm. by EMI Music Publishing). Used by permission.

I sat with a young pastor who was trying to emigrate to America. "You don't know what it's like," he said. "I've lost my job once and my wife lost her job twice because I am a pastor or I have been too aggressive. After you are beaten down so many times, you soon become afraid to do anything that may offend the KGB. I feel like an empty shell. They have killed my spirit. I know I should be doing evangelism, but I don't have the heart to try anymore. I'm just so tired."

Other pastors were making valiant efforts despite the oppressive circumstances. Yet, even these men observed great caution.

On a brisk, Sunday afternoon I sat with Yuri talking about how he was using the "JESUS" film.

"We are showing the videocassette in people's homes," he explained. "That is safer for us. You can be careful who you invite, and you can tie the showing into a birthday or an anniversary celebration."

"How do you know whether people have received Christ after the film is over?" I probed. "Can you pass out a 'comment card' or something where people can give their impressions of the film and indicate what their interest is?"

He looked at me with a benevolent smile. "No one is going to put anything about their interest in God in writing. Not in this society. If the KGB got hold of the card, it would go right in their file as evidence that they were enemies of the State."

"What do you do, then, to find out who is interested in receiving Christ?" I asked.

"I go to each one who has attended any showings held by our members to find out if they have any questions. If they are really interested, then I try to introduce them to Christ on an individual basis."

I marveled at the extreme risks he was taking for the cause of the kingdom.

Dan Peterson, who directed our ministry in this part of the world, had been there for seven years working quietly. He had gotten a teaching position in an international school, but his passion was to disciple secret believers in the evening hours. It was not easy; everything was dangerous. But when things loosened up in the future, some disciples would be there, ready to take leadership.

"Tell me about the group you have formed with new converts since the film showing," I continued with Yuri. "How many are in the group and when does it meet?"

"There are eight in the group, but the group never meets," he answered. "It would be too dangerous. There would be no way of knowing who might be ready to inform on the others. I meet with each of the members individually once a week. That way I can begin to see who is really sincere. Until I find that out, the members of my church would not even want me to invite them to come. They couldn't trust them and there would be no freedom to worship openly together."

I asked Yuri what happens when a person becomes known as a committed Christian.

"It can become very difficult for him," he said quietly. I could tell that even as he wanted to answer my question, he was not sure if he should. What if this room was bugged? Would he someday be listening to a tape of his own criticisms of the government? Would this conversation be the basis of a future prison sentence? He continued anyway.

"Once you become known as a Christian, the government begins to make life as difficult as possible for you—obviously to discourage anyone from stating that he or she is a 'believer.' He will not get an opportunity to go to the university. He will be given the worst of jobs. The government may take his children away to be sure that he is not indoctrinating them into 'Christian idealism.' And they recruit people to watch and report on the believer—sometimes even people in his own family."

I was amazed at the tenacity of the church leaders. The suffering they had gone through, and were continuing to experience, made me wonder how many people we would have in the ministry in the West if we had that kind of persecution and abuse.

I began to estimate how many videos we would need to reach the republic where Yuri lived. We would need hundreds of thousands—we'd better get started. We would need to buy videocassette recorders and blank tapes. We would need to start up an "underground" duplication facility.

We went down to the local "dollar" store. Only foreigners had the hard currency like dollars or German marks to purchase items. I went to the electronics section and bought a couple of TVs and VCRs. Then I got in line to buy forty or fifty blank videocassettes. In the next line stood another American, also buying videos.

We talked to each other in "code" for about ten minutes. He was there on an "educational exchange." I was there as a "film distributor from Hollywood" trying to do some negotiating. When we finally finished the wary circling to figure out if we could trust one another, I found out that he worked through Youth With a Mission trying to get the videos for their training base duplicated. And we set up a plan for him to get "JESUS" videos to use.

This was the situation in the Soviet Union in 1988. And it is still the situation in many other parts of the world. The people trying to show the film in restricted access countries are the pioneers for the message of Christ today. I applaud them and their courage.

At that time, though, I was troubled. This was too slow. There must be another way. Our policy in every country had been to show the "JESUS" film in conjunction with local Christians and cooperating churches. That way, new converts would have a place to go and grow in their new-found faith. But when we worked with Christians in the Soviet Union, we always put them at risk. The bolder we encouraged them to be, the more they became subject to arrest, imprisonment, or more.

We finally decided to let them take whatever risks they felt were warranted, but that we should try another way. We decided to investigate working through the government film agencies. The worst that could happen to us was that they would throw us out of the country.

With those thoughts in mind, we booked tickets and headed for Moscow—and more KGB.

As we pondered the next moves to make, I looked backward to the first breakthroughs we had in Eastern Europe. It started in Hungary with a courageous woman in the State Television Commission who had been willing to dub the "JESUS" film into the Hungarian language.

We were thrilled when the contract was signed in 1985—four years before we saw even the slightest hints of openings in the Soviet Union. We did not release any news about it, since it was such a delicate issue.

Behind the "miracle" were many faithful people who had been working for years in secret, using business covers to gain access into these Eastern European countries. Among them were Bud and Shirley Hinkson, Larry and Debbie Thompson, Andrew and Ingrid Solymosi, and many others. But in Hungary, for more than ten years, it had been Virgil Anderson, code name "Rocky."

And then the Lord raised up Edyth Bajer, the official dubbing director for Hungarian Television in Budapest.

"When the project first came to me," she said, "I knew it was something special. I didn't want to pass it on to anyone else—I wanted to do it myself. We are not in the habit of going out to look for other films to dub, but somehow I felt that my twenty-five years of dubbing experience had prepared me for just this film."

She told how everyone wanted to be involved when they heard that the film was about Jesus. "I never expected that from my colleagues. Usually, it is our job only to get the words translated, not to follow the flow of emotion. But not with this film. We first fit the Hungarian text to the lips of the actors speaking so that it seemed that the film had been made originally in Hungarian."

In their studio, they agreed not to spare any money, time, or effort to make this film as perfect as it could be. "It was not just

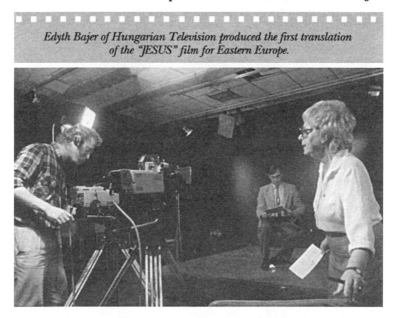

Edyth Bajer of Hungarian Television produced the first translation of the "JESUS" film for Eastern Europe.

another experience with a film, but Jesus Himself was touching us," she explained.

Normally, twenty actors are used for the dubbing. However, they used more than 150 voices. The best actors in Hungary were auditioned for the parts of Peter, James, and John. The number one actor in the country was hired to play the voice of Jesus. And, of course, for the narrator, the man who does the evening news on national television. I tried to imagine Dan Rather or Tom Brokaw narrating the "JESUS" film in English. It would be remarkable.

"And," Edyth said, "when I asked the actors to repeat their lines twenty or thirty times to be sure that they were perfect, they never complained."

For Edyth, it was more than just a project. During the dubbing of the closing prayer, she herself began to weep. And with tears of thanksgiving and joy, she received Jesus as her personal Savior and Lord.

"Before the film," Edyth recalled, "I was like everyone else. I didn't believe in Jesus, or have any faith. It wasn't a topic I even considered. I wasn't influenced by it at all. But since then it is part of my life. Never for a minute can I forget it. It has changed my life. I think everyone else feels the same way when they see this film. So many people have been influenced."

The project was so significant that the actors, for the first time in memory, came back asking to see the completed film.

"When I started to show it inside the TV company," she said, "it wasn't easy for the workers to come and see it. It was not politically advisable for them to see a film like this. But slowly people came because the room was dark. At the end, everyone was crying." For Edyth and a lot of actors in a Communist country, this film was a "special gift of God to the Hungarian people."

Within months, the "JESUS" video was selling in government shops, and by the end of the year it had become the number one seller in the country. One government official thought this was especially curious, since the majority of people owning VCRs were Communist Party members.

A Gospel of Luke booklet, with illustrated pictures taken from the film, was released, and it sold more than 150,000 copies in the first three weeks. All of this was taking place when any missionary work going on in the country was illegal.

However, God was at work. We obtained permission to import three 16mm films for the express purpose of showing them to Catholic school children. Soon the Hungarian University students in Budapest began to hear about the film and asked to use it. They refused to be stopped. They took it everywhere. The Good News had to be spread.

In my initial experience with these students in 1987, the situation at first looked as repressive as you could imagine. They took me to a crowded upstairs apartment in Budapest. The night sky and cold rain reminded me of a spy movie. In the spy movies I've seen, it's always raining. Nobody smiles. The situation is gloomy and depressing.

But this was not a spy movie. And the room was not gloomy. It was alive and vibrant and filled with hope! I sat with twenty-five college students talking about the impact of the "JESUS" film.

"Why are college students so interested in seeing this film?" I asked a twenty-year-old. "You get all the latest Hollywood movies here. The 'JESUS' film doesn't have any car chases or big action scenes. Why do all these students want to see it?"

He looked at me, slowly shaking his head. "You don't understand, do you? You see, we've never had a film in this country about *God*. We've always been able to see films, but never a film that tells you how you can know God! I'm going to see it for the thirtieth time this weekend!"

A few hours earlier, I had seen this same curiosity and interest over at the university. As my host and I approached the dormitory, he said, "Just act like you live here." I wiped some more lint on my pants, messed up my hair, wrinkled my khaki jacket, and tried to look bored. At least that was how I thought most Eastern European college students looked.

We made it past the government security people who could have asked us for our student IDs, but didn't. As we arrived at the elevator of the ten-story dormitory, we saw on the wall above the elevator door a poster announcing the coming film showing. Someone had hung one on every floor.

As the 8 p.m. meeting time approached, groups of students, five or six at a time, entered the lounge. Most of them were men.

Within minutes more than a hundred were there. Students started sitting on the floor, filling the aisles.

Tears came to my eyes. This was a Communist country. Christian evangelistic meetings were not permitted. But no system of government can ever quench the hunger of the human heart to know God.

Now here I was in this room of college students listening to the report of the film showings. In the first showing on one university campus, the response had been awesome. Crowds of fifty and a hundred soon grew until at one showing more than a thousand saw the film.

From the campuses, the college students started taking the film to their hometowns on the weekends. A woman in the Catholic church showed me on her calendar where all three films they had were booked every night for the next seven months. "Please get us more copies," she begged.

One student told of some village showings where the older women got down under the pews during the beatings of Jesus. They were so frightened that they were unable to watch the horror on the screen.

As the students told about the showings, they reported a wonderful response. There were always tears, always people sitting in stunned silence, always people indicating that they had received Christ.

"How do you find out what the response is?" I asked the students.

"We pass out a little comment sheet," one replied, "so we can find out what they thought about the film. About 70 percent of those who see the film will fill out the comment paper. We ask them things like:

'What did you think of the film?'

'What parts did you like the best?'

'Did you pray the prayer at the end to receive Christ as your personal Savior?'"

"How many indicate that they prayed the prayer to receive Christ?" I asked.

"Most of the people do," they answered. As I quizzed them some more, I found that as many as 70 percent of those who turned in their comments indicated that they had received Christ.

That would mean 70 percent of the 70 percent, or about half of some groups, indicated a decision to receive Christ.

Why are they so responsive? I wondered.

The next night brought some answers. I met with forty lay people who had been involved in showing the film in homes and parishes. Some were Catholic, some were Protestant. For security reasons, they had never been together before.

Since the coming of freedom to Eastern Europe, it is difficult to capture adequately the intense pressures under which some of those earlier showings took place. In restricted countries, the secret police constantly monitored every kind of religious group activity. Christian people who showed the film risked harassment; loss of jobs, positions, and apartments; and sometimes they were sent to prison.

While some countries now are loosening the restrictions, others are tightening them. Even within the same country we find ebbs and flows of religious freedom. The biggest opponents to the spread of the "JESUS" film continue to be the remaining hardline Communist countries and a number of Islamic republics and states.

The older people remembered being taken as children to mass or church, singing hymns, and praying before Communists took over their country. Then most of the churches were closed, and if people attended the remaining churches, they could not be Party members. They would be socially ostracized and ridiculed. So they gave up their faith.

Now, forty years later, as they watch the "JESUS" film, they are overcome with emotion. Many weep. The memories of childhood, of a simple belief in God, of a mother or a grandmother who taught them to pray—all of those come flooding back. They realize the barrenness of spirit and the emptiness of hollow, secular mankind, and with great gratitude, they open their lives to the Lord.

■ ■ ■ ■ ■

Back in my room in Moscow, I prayed for a little crack in the Iron Curtain such as we had seen just months before in Hungary. "Lord, give us an opportunity. You open the door."

Jaan Heinmets, my host on the trip, said, "We should go to the Republic of Georgia. People say that they are the great black marketeers of the Soviet Union. Maybe we can figure a good way to get the 'JESUS' film into the black market."

Some earlier forays into Tbilisi by some of our Hungarian contacts indicated that the Georgian Film Studio might be open to a similar arrangement to dub the film as we had in Hungary. We flew to Georgia.

Our contact was Vaso Margvelashvili, a smooth, wily, chain-smoking, Georgian businessman. The subject matter, a Christian film, was a little outside his comfort zone. But as a shrewd businessman, he would make a great effort to deliver on his promise to help get negotiations going in his city. Like all influential Georgians at that time, he had contacts everywhere: the Communist Party, the Orthodox Church, Georgian government leaders, and those who knew how to get things done.

We drove down Rustaveli Prospect. The leaves on the trees made a beautiful canopy over the road, pale golden-green in the afternoon sun. What a refreshing relief from Moscow!

Our contact took me directly to see the head of the Georgian Film Studio, Rezo Chkeidze.

"My name is Paul Eshleman," I began. "I am the president of a film company from California. I am here to investigate whether we might come to some agreement with you to dub a film on the life of Jesus into the Georgian language and show it in your public theaters. We know you have a Christian heritage in Georgia, and that is why we have come here first."

"Please let me welcome you," he smiled. "What you are talking about is of great interest to us."

And so began the negotiations. It was against the law for Soviet citizens to receive dollars for anything. And rubles were not attractive at all. Nothing could be bought with rubles. We found ourselves paying for taxis with small American gifts and talking about how to trade technical equipment for their labor. After three days of meetings, we signed a letter of agreement stating that we would give them a one-hundred-year lease on a piece of equipment in exchange for their dubbing and distributing the film in the Georgian language.

That night, some local Christians came to talk privately.

"Don't you know," they whispered, "that Rezo is KGB?"

"No, I didn't know that," I answered. "But if he can help us get the film translated, and we can be guaranteed that the script will not be altered in any way, then we will work with him. I understand that it might be better for you if you are not seen with us. That's okay. We don't want you to be endangered in any way. But why don't we carefully try to get you a copy of the script after it is translated into Georgian? You can help make sure that the Scripture has not been changed."

It seemed unusual to depend on a KGB man to help get the film into the Soviet Union. On the other hand, God opens doors, and He determines whom He will use to accomplish His will. During the next two years, Rezo would do more than any other man to help bring the "JESUS" film to Georgia and ultimately to the entire Soviet Union.

It would take sixteen months to complete the translation, dubbing, and production of the film. But that next trip to Georgia became one of the most memorable of my life...

CHAPTER 3

An Unbelievable Event in Soviet Georgia

D ecember 8, 1989. We were met at the plane by the KGB and government leaders; they did not follow us—they gave us a police escort! Official cars, with loudspeakers blaring and sirens wailing, led our black Chaika limousine through the winding streets of Tbilisi to the largest theater in Georgia.

The lights of the Philharmonic Hall sparkled like gems in the night. Parking facilities were overrun; cars spilled over onto all the sidewalks in the surrounding areas. Government officials, Communist Party members, and special guests had long since filled the 2,300 seats of the concert hall. The spaces on every step and in all the aisles were taken by those who had managed to talk their way past the security guards.

This was an unbelievable event—an impossible event! The theatrical premiere of the "JESUS" film in the Soviet Union, the "evil empire"! This was the country that had killed millions in Siberian labor camps, persecuted countless Christians, and forbade teaching children about Jesus. This was the nation that gave us the KGB, the Cold War, and the corrupt Communist Party.

Now, here in the birthplace of its most vicious leader, Joseph Stalin, here in Tbilisi in the Republic of Georgia, for the first time, a Christian film was opening in a theater in the Soviet Union!

A back door opened.

"Quickly, please. Put your coats here," an official of the Georgian Film Studio instructed. After a few hurried introductions, our party was led backstage.

37

Tbilisi, Georgia. The Philharmonic Hall, the round building in the top center of the photo, was the site of the premiere.

More instructions on the processional order, and we were led on stage for the opening ceremonies by His Holiness and Beatitude Catholicos Ilia II, head of the Georgian Orthodox Church.

The first public showing of a Christian film in the history of the Soviet Union.

As we emerged from the wings to center stage, the audience stood in thundering ovation. The anticipation and excitement in the air was absolutely electric.

"Ladies and gentlemen, welcome to the premiere of 'JESUS,' the first film of its kind ever to be dubbed and shown in the Soviet Union." English-speaking interpreters repeated for us the words of emcee Vaso Margvelashvili, director of the premiere. The applause overwhelmed us as one by one the honored guests rose to greet the crowd.

The Catholicos was introduced first. The Patriarch

and his priests had approved the translation of the script. Dressed in the traditional black robes, with a cross adorning the miter of his hat and a scepter in his hand, the Catholicos rose to give his blessing to the film. For most Georgians, he is a symbol not only of the Church, but also of their people and culture. With genuine, sincere words, he praised the film for its accuracy and faithfulness to St. Luke's Gospel. The audience burst into warm and loving applause.

Next came introductions of those from the Georgian Film Studio who had worked with our technician to produce the Georgian translation: the actor who had dubbed the voice of Jesus; the director, Soso; and the head of the studio, Rezo Chkeidze.

Then someone introduced me.

"It is one of the great honors and privileges of my life to celebrate this wonderful evening with you," I began. In every respect, I truly meant those words. To see this film shown in the Soviet Union was a dream wonderfully coming true.

"Tonight, I want to tell you a little bit about this unique film that you are about to see. It is perhaps the most accurate film ever produced on the life of Jesus." I paused periodically for my interpreter. "Five years of research came before the actual camera work began.

"Each scene was filmed in the Holy Land," I explained, "as close as possible to the very site where the event took place nearly two thousand years ago.

"All of the cloth was handwoven, because that's what they did then." The crowd listened attentively as I explained how drawings of Hebrew slaves found in Egyptian pyramids determined the designs of the clothing. "Only thirty-three colors were used," I said, "because those were the only dyes available in the first century. The fish you see in the film were caught in the Sea of Galilee. And the words Jesus speaks are all found in the Holy Scriptures."

"'JESUS' is now the most translated film in the history of the motion picture business," I said. "Completed translations now number 145, and the film has been seen by 330 million people in 166 countries."

I paused for a moment to let the interpreter catch up. "Tonight, I want to pay a special tribute to Mr. Rezo Chkeidze who had the courage to be the first studio director in the Soviet Union to translate a Christian film. May God bless all of you tonight as you watch the film."

After the applause died down, I continued, "Now it is my very great pleasure to present the first copy of the 'JESUS' film in the Georgian language to His Holiness and Beatitude Catholicos Ilia II."

He came forward to receive the film along with one of the coffee table books on the "JESUS" film filled with pictures from the film. The plates for this book had been mistakenly destroyed by the publisher, and this was one of the few remaining copies.

Another resounding ovation. And then, the remaining three members of our U.S. contingent on the program were introduced: Ohio Congressman, the Honorable Bob McEwen; USAF Major General John Jackson from the Pentagon; and Nelson "Bud" Hinkson, director of all the Campus Crusade ministries in Eastern Europe for twenty years. All were warmly received.

Paul Eshleman presents the first copy of the "JESUS" film in the Georgian language to Rezo Chkeidze, director of the Georgian Film Studio; His Holiness Ilia II of the Georgian Orthodox Church; and the actor who dubbed the voice of Jesus.

The emcee asked, "How many of you have ever seen an American general here in the Soviet Union in person?" Not one person raised a hand.

"It is my privilege to introduce now, traveling in an unofficial capacity, U.S. Air Force Major General John Jackson, from the Pentagon in Washington."

Gasps went up and a low rumble of excited whispers spread across the crowd as the general walked to the microphone. Here in front of them was one of the hated "American imperialist warmongers." Here was a general from Washington, D.C., who was "building more weapons and threatening the peace of the world." That is what they had been told.

General Jackson, a humble, gracious man of God, was the first of the three to speak. As he stepped to the microphone dressed in a civilian suit, he projected the image of a kind and gentle spirit. Had he worn his uniform, the audience would have seen half the chest of his jacket lined with medals: one for flying 398 combat missions in Vietnam; the Distinguished Flying Cross; the Bronze Star; the Legion of Merit; and on and on.

"I have spent the major portion of my life preparing for war," John began. *Mostly for war with the Soviet Union,* I thought, but he didn't say that.

"But while being a soldier has been my career and occupation, in my heart I have prayed for peace." Applause. "It may interest you to know that I am part of a group of twenty-five generals and admirals who meet each week in the Pentagon to pray for peace. We pray for ourselves and our families, and we have been praying for you."

Again, the people interrupted him with enthusiastic applause, looking at one another in amazement.

"The film you will see tonight is about Jesus, the Prince of Peace. I have come to the Soviet Union as a private citizen simply to encourage those of you who have found greater meaning in your life through faith in Jesus."

The applause was long and enthusiastic. The crowd seemed to sense that this was a significant happening, a unique night in the history of a republic that had known great pain.

Only a few months before, protestors against the "Soviet occupation of Georgia" had been clubbed to death in the town square.

More than four thousand people had been overcome by poisonous gas, shot into the crowd by Soviet troops flown in from Moscow. The burning fire of nationalistic independence raged in this republic's bosom.

Next, Congressman McEwen strode to the microphone. At six-foot-four, with a booming orator's voice, he was an imposing presence. But this was not a political speech. These people couldn't vote for him, or anybody else for that matter.

"I count it one of the great privileges of my life to be with you at this time. I was invited to have dinner tonight at the White House with the President of the United States, but I turned down that invitation so I might be with you, the people of Georgia, on this very special occasion."

Pausing for the interpreter, he continued, "We have been watching the events taking place here in Tbilisi. Tonight I salute you for your courage and your convictions. God bless you and God bless Georgia!"

The ovation again filled the hall. Traditionally Christian, the Georgians had long chafed under Soviet dominance. Their churches are filled with holy relics that they believe once belonged to the apostles. According to their tradition, the Virgin Mother watches over Georgia and actually sent two of the disciples to the Caucasus Mountains to bring the gospel to this ancient people. They believe that Christ's robe was brought to Georgia after His burial; a church stands today on the site where it was buried, along with the woman who brought it.

Georgians are an emotional people with fiery temperaments. For centuries, they have fought for survival against the Turkish Muslims. Millions have died in their struggle to save both their country and their faith. For many, God and country are inextricably linked.

So this premiere was more than just the showing of a film. It was a statement to Moscow.

"This film is in our language, and it is about God," they seemed to be saying. "These are our roots, our heritage. Communist rule will never kill our spirit. For seventy years you have not permitted us to teach our children about God. You have closed our cathedrals and ridiculed our faith. But tonight we show this film, and we tell you, 'We believe in God!'"

During the next few moments, others were introduced. Then I was presented with a gold medallion on a chain, on which the word for *Jesus* in the Georgian language had been designed in the form of a cross. It was beautiful, and I felt deeply touched.

The time came for the prayer of dedication by Bud Hinkson, long-time pioneer of the ministry in Eastern Europe. Then the lights were lowered. We were ushered to reserved seats in the middle of the huge hall. Because people filled every available space, we had to thread our way carefully.

As we watched the film in the darkened theater, I thought about the early beginnings of the project. I was amazed again as I recalled the miracles that had taken place in order to bring the "JESUS" film to fruition. The idea originated many years ago in the heart and mind of Dr. Bill Bright, founder and president of Campus Crusade for Christ International, the sponsoring organization.

For years, Dr. Bright had cherished a dream of having a film on the life of Christ available to help bring people to the Savior. At one time he approached the famous filmmaker Cecil B.

Production crew scene of Jesus walking with the rich young ruler in the desert outside Jerusalem.

"JESUS" film producer, John Heyman

DeMille to see what could be done. Financing was always a problem, and it persistently delayed the project.

In 1976, in God's timing, all the elements seemed to come together. A British film producer, John Heyman, approached Dr. Bright with the idea of producing a film on the life of Jesus. Bunker and Caroline Hunt agreed to put up the needed six million dollars, and I formed a company, called Inspirational Films and later The JESUS Film Project, to handle worldwide translation and distribution.

The film opened in two thousand theaters in North America in the fall of 1979. More than six hundred local volunteer committees were established throughout the country to help sell tickets in advance of the opening at the box office. Warner Brothers handled the theatrical release, and the film began to appear on HBO, Showtime, and other cable channels. But from the beginning, it was intended to be a film for the entire world.

Every care was taken during the research and development of the film to keep it as faithful as possible to the Scriptures. For authenticity, the film would be shot in Israel. A 150-page research document was prepared. Every character who would eventually appear in the film was listed, along with the number of scenes in which they would appear. General notes were made for the casting director to help him find the right kind of people, and for the wardrobe and make-up directors so they would know how each character should look.

Six months before the shooting began, one assistant director traveled to several Israeli villages to enlist men to begin growing beards for the film. It saved time and money not having to paste false beards on thousands of men when we filmed the feeding of the five thousand.

Other parts of the research document described the towns that would be shown:

Galilean towns were well-populated, with populations as large as a thousand. The Gentile population was twice as large as the Jewish population. Streets were narrow passageways between houses of mud-dried bricks. The streets would have been crooked, with refuse well trampled into the dirt and no paving or cobble stones. None of the stone Herodian-built towns were visited by Jesus in the Luke account.

Sixteen pages of research were devoted to the description of the Temple, the Temple Mount, the dimensions of each of the courts in and around the Temple, and the wardrobe of the priests. In fact, months of research went into determining just how each of the characters should be dressed. What colors should the tunics be? How should the large tallith be depicted for the Pharisees? How should the soldiers be dressed? What would a beggar have worn?

A potter was brought in to duplicate the hundreds of pots of all sizes that would be needed for the various scenes—water jars, wine pitchers, oil juglets, large storage urns, beakers, fish-plates, and Megarian bowls.

Paul Eshleman's role as a Roman soldier lasted only three seconds.

I thought about all the work that had gone into the production of the film. I would not have known the difference between the bowls. I really didn't know how people dressed or looked in those days. But the researchers did. And they had spared no expense to make this film as realistic as humanly possible. For me, it was gratifying that such care had been taken to ensure the pictorial accuracy of the film.

■ ■ ■ ■ ■

The rising crescendo of music jerked me back to the present and I realized that we were nearing the conclusion of the film. *What will happen when the evangelistic presentation at the end comes on?* I

wondered. *Will people walk out?* We hadn't been able to show that
closing invitation in the United States release. Warner Brothers
had agreed to distribute the film to the theaters but had said,
"We're not going to show the 'commercial for God' at the end!"
Now here we were in the Soviet Union, preparing to include the
invitation to receive Christ right on the film.

I began to pray.

As the invitation was shown, the audience sat in rapt silence.
No one moved. Then, during the prayer of repentance, I could
hear people weeping, and a soft murmur rose as they repeated
the prayer of invitation to receive Christ. When it was over, the
audience stood to their feet applauding. The applause soon
turned into the rhythmic clapping of "we want more." When they
spotted our delegation in the middle of the hall, they all turned
toward us smiling and applauding. We waved to them, and the
applause grew louder. No one moved until we had been led
through the crowd to the lobby.

In the lobby, full-blown chaos enveloped us. I had brought two
thousand color pictures of Jesus holding a little child, with each
enclosed in a white folder. Printed across the front of the picture
was "Jesus" in the Georgian language. People besieged us, asking
for pictures and autographs.

Others who had seen the film just squeezed our hands, tears
streaming from their eyes, unable to speak. As leaders in the
Communist Party, these people had not been permitted to know
God. A young man about twenty-five grabbed my hand and wept,
pointing to his heart. This film was touching people to the depths
of their souls.

One of the older leaders, unashamed of the tears rolling down
his cheeks, appeared before me. "I am eighty-four years old," his
voice quavered, "and this has been the most powerful and the
most meaningful two hours of my entire life."

We needed a hundred counselors! We needed Bibles, discipleship materials, group leaders, new pastors, more churches. We
had very few; still, we had begun!

This night the angels would rejoice—but none of them more
than I.

CHAPTER 4

One Awesome, Powerful, Unforgettable Moment

A few hours later, sunshine streamed through the trees warming the rooftops as Tbilisi awoke to a Sunday morning. It is a picturesque city, surrounded by mountains whose peaks reach into the clouds. For those of us who attended the "JESUS" film premiere, it had been a short night. At midnight we gathered to give thanks for the privilege of being a part of such a historic occasion. Seeing the hand of God at work like this, opening doors and touching lives, humbled us.

This morning, with our police escort in place, we headed off to worship at the Baptist Church. None of our hosts had ever visited the Baptist Church—they were all atheists or Orthodox—and the police escort had to stop and ask for directions! The whole caravan of cars and buses made a U-turn in the street and headed down a small alley toward the church.

We intended simply to join the Russian language service at 10 a.m. and then be on our way to the Sioni Cathedral where the Catholicos would celebrate a high mass at noon in our honor.

But the Baptist Church officials apparently knew we were coming and led us directly to the platform where chairs awaited us. They quickly whispered to us that the general and congressman would be giving their testimonies and that I would be giving the sermon. Alexi Bichkoff, secretary of the All-Union Baptist Churches, would be my interpreter.

Until recently, instructing the children in the Christian faith was illegal before they had completed school, and by that time, few of them sought out God or the church. In the last few years, though, the numbers of young people have begun to grow.

So now, as with all of their Baptist churches, the front pews were reserved for the elderly. Older women with their head scarves and heavy coats outnumbered the men about ten to one.

One old man on the front row wore a coat pinned with war medals. He had fought in World War II, and now, by wearing his medals, he could ride the subway free and go to the front of any line. Since people stand in line to buy almost everything, this was an important consideration.

A church elder sat at a table on the platform next to me, collecting little notes that were brought to the front by various people. The notes, I learned, were specific requests for prayer.

I spoke on Matthew 24:14: "This gospel of the kingdom will be preached in the whole world as a testimony to all the nations, and then the end will come." This chapter is one of the most exciting in all of the Bible. Jesus told His disciples that just before His physical return to earth, everyone would hear the gospel, the "good news" of His love and forgiveness. By the grace of God, He seems to be using the "JESUS" film as one of those ways in which many people can hear.

I told this congregation about Maasai warriors coming to Christ in Africa, of Muslims in Indonesia, and Buddhists in Thailand. They were especially moved when they heard of the tremendous growth of the church in Nepal despite the fact that being baptized means a year's sentence in prison.

I looked down at the audience and wondered what sacrifices they had made to keep worshipping these many years. I glanced over at the Georgian entourage and wondered what they were thinking. I realized that the reporters, drivers, interpreters, and helpers who had accompanied us had never before been in a Baptist or Protestant church. Later, as we drove to the next meeting, they told me how impressed they were. This was the first time they ever heard anyone teach from the Bible.

We finished the service and were preparing to leave when the pastor rushed up to say that we "must" greet the people now coming in for the Georgian language service. We tried to explain that we were due at the Cathedral in a few minutes, but they prevailed on us to stay for fifteen more minutes. I spoke briefly.

"During the last two nights, in the Philharmonic Hall, we premiered the 'JESUS' film in the Georgian language," I began. "Many important guests were there, including government leaders. Now the film will be showing in theaters all over Georgia."

The audience applauded and chattered among themselves as if they couldn't believe that the film was in Georgian, and that it would be shown in their cities.

When I continued, "At this time, I want to present your pastor with a copy of the video in the Georgian language," they applauded again.

The pastor asked when they could get the 16mm film. I responded thoughtfully, "By Easter, I hope."

It was now 12:15, and we were running very late for our appearance at the Orthodox Cathedral. The police escort hustled us across town, and the crowd at the Sioni Cathedral parted to let us walk down to the front. In Orthodox churches, people stand for the entire service. But for us, ten chairs were placed next to the altar.

The cathedral was beautiful, built as all Orthodox churches in the shape of a cross, with high ceilings as if to open up more of the heavens to the worshippers. Each prayer is lifted upward along with symbolic incense. Candles burn in rows in front of icons—statues of various saints and of the Virgin Mother and Jesus. We each were given candles to light and place in front of the icon of Jesus.

The liturgy continued for the next half-hour. I looked at a woman nearby, kissing the image of Jesus, tears streaming down her cheeks. Praise, worship, adoration, and devotion shone from her face.

Not accustomed to this liturgical form and unable to understand the language, we watched carefully to know when to stand, kneel, or bow. Then the Catholicos came from behind the closed section of the altar and a podium was brought and placed in front of him.

His expression was animated and warm as he began, "I want to welcome to Sioni Cathedral today these special guests from the United States of America." He introduced us quickly. Again, a murmur raced through the crowd as people strained to see which one of us was the American general.

"These people have brought to us a wonderful film on the life of Jesus. It was translated into Georgian here in our own film studios," the patriarch announced. "I had a chance to see it before in English and Russian, but when I heard Jesus speaking Georgian, I knew the film was for us." Applause rang throughout the cathedral.

"Last night we had the premiere of the film here in Georgia at the Philharmonic Hall," he continued. "As I watched the film, I was struck in my heart by the scene in which Peter denies our Lord three times. After the third denial, the cock crows and Peter suddenly realizes what he has done. When Jesus looks at him, Peter is overcome with grief at his sins."

The Catholicos spoke with conviction. "All of us need to repent of our sins so that we will not be ashamed when Jesus looks at us. We need a new revival! We need a renaissance of faith in our hearts. This film, 'JESUS,' can help to bring that to our country."

He then asked me to come up on the podium. He kissed me on the right cheek, gave me a hug, and invited me to speak.

"I greet you in the name of the risen Lord Jesus," I began. There was no loudspeaker system, and the people in the back yelled out that they couldn't hear when my Georgian interpreter spoke too quietly. He accommodated them and spoke up.

I gave a little background on the film, told them that it would soon be playing the theaters, and once again commended the people of Georgia for their courage in translating and showing this film on the life of Jesus.

We then were presented with lovely gifts by the Catholicos. I received a copper engraving of "The Last Supper" and some beautiful books.

Then the Patriarch stepped behind the altar and emerged with a beautiful new Bible.

"I am holding before you the first copy of the Holy Scriptures in the modern Georgian language," he beamed. "It was just completed this week after twelve years of work."

Applause resounded throughout the cathedral. The Catholicos held the book high over his head, then pointed it in each direction. The audience bowed toward the Scriptures as they passed in front.

Speaking loudly, he continued with his speech. "We will have 25,000 of these available for you to buy this year. That is very few for so many who will want to buy these Scriptures.

"The wonderful thing about this Bible is how understandable it is. As you know, the text of our previous Bible was translated in the twelfth century. Because so many words have changed in our modern Georgian language, it has been difficult for us to understand.

"I hope each of you can get a Bible, and I want you to read it twice a day."

The choir began to sing one of the most beautiful melodies I have ever heard. As they repeated the refrain, we began to hum along with the choir.

"What is that anthem about?" I whispered to an interpreter behind me.

"It's about life eternal," he whispered.

My eyes filled with tears as I lifted my heart in praise and worship to the Lord.

I was not the only one with tears. We were in the presence of the Lord—Americans and citizens of the Soviet Union, who had been enemies for decades, speaking different languages, from very different confessional backgrounds. Here together, we were witnessing the culmination of the working of the Spirit of God to bring the message of His love and forgiveness to a generation in the USSR who knew little of His message.

Who could have planned this? Who could have orchestrated these elements? Bible translators from Sweden worked with Georgian Orthodox theologians for twelve years. Government officials granted permission for importing the Bibles. Fund-raising from somewhere covered the costs.

And on our side, what a chain of events: an initial contact with the film studio by a German-speaking Hungarian who had studied in the Soviet Union, my own trip to negotiate the contract, a dubbing team of technicians sent to do the work, provision of funds by Norma Alloway.

I remembered her call two years before on New Year's Eve. "I want to help translate the 'JESUS' film for several parts of the world," she said. "Which languages would you recommend?" She and her family provided the funds for seven languages, one of them Georgian.

When the translation was completed, new titles in Georgian prepared, and the premiere set up, the church I attend in California provided the funds for the premiere. In the first few days, twelve thousand viewers would attend. And now, in the very same week, the modern Bible in Georgian was finished.

And all this happened in the climate of *glasnost* and *perestroika*, the week after Gorbachev had met with the Pope, the week after his announcement that there would be "freedom of conscience" for people to worship as they please.

Behind all this outward activity, people had been praying and pleading with a sovereign God for the citizens of the Soviet Union. Even now, thousands of people were praying for this trip, as they had promised to do.

How desperately I longed for my wife, my son, and my daughter to share these moments. I wanted them to experience and understand with me just a little of how great, how powerful, and how utterly incomprehensible is God's love for the world. This was God at work—and He let us see it and be involved in it.

As Christians, we are involved in a commission and a vision, a cause that gives meaning and purpose to our lives. "This is what we are about as a family," I wanted to tell our children. "This is why your mother and I do what we do. Whatever your vocation in life, don't forget the cause of the kingdom!"

"The cause of the kingdom"—that had been my motivation for more than twenty-five years. Of all the challenges given to men and women throughout the centuries, is there any that compares to taking the message of Jesus to the world? I can think of nothing that would even come close.

I had prepared for a life in business and completed my MBA in marketing and finance when someone asked me about my purpose in life. I read a passage in the Scriptures where Jesus said, "Where your treasure is, there your heart will be also" (Luke 12:34). I began to realize for the first time that I really had made my own plan for my life—then asked God to put His blessing on it. I wanted Jesus as my Savior, but I wanted to run my own life.

That night I read 2 Timothy 2:4: "No one serving as a soldier gets involved in civilian affairs—he wants to please his commanding officer."

In the darkness of the early hours of the morning, I knelt by my bed and began discussing my life with the Lord. I told Him I wanted to start working toward things that would count eternally. I recalled the plaque on my grandmother's wall:

Only one life, 'twill soon be past.
Only what's done for Christ will last.

I told the Lord that I didn't want to be entangled in the affairs of this life. I wanted to lay up my treasure in heaven. And I wanted to present myself to God to do whatever He wanted to with me. I would go wherever He wanted me to go, and give away whatever He wanted me to give away. That morning I gave my life totally and completely to Him. And I found tremendous freedom.

Now, years later, I was privileged to be taking this incredible film to countries all over the world. It would give hundreds of millions of people the chance to see how wonderful Jesus really is. It would help many millions of people each year to come into the family of God. These people were going to live forever. What greater cause could there ever be to live for? I could be involved, even if only a little, in the same cause that sent Jesus into the world: to help men and women be brought back to God and live eternally with Him.

All these thoughts raced through my mind as the triumphant anthem of the choir resounded across the cathedral. We were a most privileged group of people. In the eternal plan of the ages, we were being allowed to see—even for just a microsecond—the power, the impact, and the wonder of the God of the universe working all things together for His glory.

I remembered the words of Dennis Kinlaw from Asbury Seminary: "Give me one divine moment when God acts, and I say that that moment is far superior to all the efforts of mankind throughout the centuries." This was certainly one of those moments—Spirit-filled, awesome, powerful, and absolutely unforgettable!

CHAPTER 5

Go for It!

As the new decade began in 1990, we were still rejoicing over the opening of the film in Soviet Georgia. Each visit to the country revealed more and more openness. Everything was changing so rapidly that no one knew for sure what was or was not possible.

In early February, I assembled our leaders in The JESUS Film Project. "Let's see if we can duplicate what has happened in Georgia in every republic of the USSR and in every country of Eastern Europe."

I outlined the plan. We would divide into teams of two, create a travel schedule, and start negotiations in all twenty-three areas by the end of May, just three months away.

"If we do not have the language translated for that republic or country, we'll attempt to sign a contract to dub it in their national studio," I instructed. "If we have the language dubbed, we'll check to be sure it is done well enough to place in their commercial theaters. If it is not, we'll sign a contract to dub it again." (We had dubbed some of the Iron Curtain languages already available with refugees living in the United States and some of them had lost their pure accent.)

"If we have the dubbed film ready," I continued, "we'll attempt to sign a distribution contract to show the film in their theaters, and eventually on their national television. We'll design generic contracts, translate these into Russian, and start trying to set up appointments with film studios in all these places."

It was an exciting time. Schedules had to be changed. Current projects put on hold. Tasks divided up. Territories assigned.

Stephen Freed and I would take Bulgaria, Czechoslovakia, Romania, and three republics in the USSR: Russia, Latvia, and Azerbaijan. Stephen would make a second trip to Poland, East

Germany, and Hungary. Bob Bradberry and Matt Prochaska would cover Estonia, Lithuania, Belarus, Moldavia, the Ukraine, and Yugoslavia. Dave Scott and Alex Thompson would begin negotiations in the tough Muslim republics of Uzbekistan, Kazakhstan, and Kyrgyzstan. Ronnie Deans and Ron Green were assigned to Turkmenistan and Armenia. The entire project would eventually number thirty-five languages, each for more than one million people, and scores of contracts.

We bought the plane tickets and began to look for contacts to meet the right people, get visas, and find interpreters. Mostly, we prayed and looked at maps. It's hard to know how to begin if you aren't even sure where you're going. Where exactly is Kazakhstan and does *anyone* we know have a contact there?

We went as representatives of a film company to make a business deal. It was a good decision. Business they understood. Missions was not an option, especially in the Muslim areas. We met together as a team. What would we offer? How could we make our deal attractive? Why should a Soviet government film studio in a Shiite Muslim republic be interested in dubbing and distributing a film about Jesus?

In every place, businesses were desperate for dollars. So we offered five thousand dollars to each film company that would translate the film into the language of that country or republic. We also offered to pay for the film copies in most areas, something not usually done by a film company, and then promised to split the profits. They could not lose on the business part of it.

But making a profit was a new concept to most of those with whom we dealt. Furthermore, for seventy years, the government had controlled everything. If a film studio suffered a loss, the government covered it. If the studio earned a profit, the government took it. So the question became: Would a studio director just decide to show the "JESUS" film or not?

I assigned myself Bulgaria. Outside of Albania, it was known as the toughest country in the Eastern Bloc. We had no contacts. Advisors told me not to go. Nothing would happen, they said. But I told the travel folks to book the flight.

While speaking to a group of college students in Chicago, I mentioned that I wanted to go to Bulgaria. A young student came up afterward. "I am really excited about what you said regarding

Bulgaria," he smiled. "My parents work there in the American Embassy. I'm sure they'll help you!" And they did.

A few weeks before we were to leave, I received a call from a good friend in New York City, B. J. Weber. His wife, Sheila, had played a small part in the "JESUS" film. "Paul, I've been ministering to the ambassador to the U.N. from Bulgaria. Do you have the film in the Bulgarian language that I can give to him?" he asked.

"I'm planning to go to Sofia in a few weeks to start the negotiations to dub the film there," I replied.

"Well," B. J. continued, "this man has just been appointed the vice president in the new government. Maybe he can help you. He returns to his country next week."

Two weeks later we sat in a private dining room in Bulgaria with B. J. and the vice president, talking about the changes taking place in the government.

"We face great challenges," the vice president lamented. "We want to change to a free market society, but where do we start? If we want to sell the factories to private parties, who has enough money to buy them?"

We talked of many things. Then he said, "You might be interested to know about a survey we took recently in this country. We found that 50 percent of the people believe in God."

Paul Eshleman (left) and B. J. Weber (right) meet with the vice president of Bulgaria, A. Semmerdzhler, who helped them open the doors for showing the film in his country.

It was true. The night before, I had seen first-hand the hunger of the people. We had been invited to the flat of some employees of the American Embassy to meet with a few pastors. It was not something the embassy officials would have been especially happy about. Employees are warned against any kind of religious activities involving nationals. Still, they wanted their friends to know that the film might eventually be available in Bulgarian.

One hostess had cautioned, "Don't say anything here that you don't want the Bulgarians to know. I'm sure our apartments are bugged."

"It's okay," I assured her. "We are dealing very openly with the officials. We have nothing to hide."

One of the pastors had brought an interpreter, a new graduate of language school who was intrigued by the subject matter. After we had exchanged greetings, she said, "I will be happy to go outside if you want to tell secrets about the church." There was openness, apparently, but the local people were not fully buying it yet.

After dinner, we showed about thirty minutes of the film, including the death and resurrection of Jesus. Since we only had it in Russian, she was translating for the Bulgarian pastors and their wives.

During the crucifixion scenes her voice started to break. Tears filled her eyes. Deeply moved, she could not go on.

But that was last night. Now we were with the vice president, hoping to open the doors a little wider.

Twenty-four thousand people saw the "JESUS" film during the first month it opened in Bulgaria.

Finally, about 2:30, he said, "You'll have to excuse me now. This afternoon we are going to change the name of the Communist Party." These were momentous days. We were experiencing history in the making.

The next morning we had our second meeting with Lyudmil Staikov, president of the Bulgarian Film Studio and member of the Communist Party. As we began the meeting, he passed across his desk a newspaper.

"Here is the last copy of the *Communist Daily Worker*. This paper was started in 1927. This is the last issue. Yesterday they changed the name of the Communist Party.

"Last night I watched your film," he continued. "Frankly, I didn't like it."

I tried to keep the smile from fading from my face. Inside I was praying. *What do we do next,* I wondered. *What should I say?* We would have to go forward some other way. The Bulgarian Film Studio might say no, but it didn't change things. We would have to find another way to translate the film. If they wouldn't distribute the film, we would have to find another way to do that, too. Jesus commanded us to take the gospel everywhere. If we smuggled videos into the country, it would still be possible for millions to see the film—if we could get it translated into Bulgarian.

"Is there any way you might be willing to at least do the dubbing?" I asked.

"Well," he shrugged, "I've been thinking about it, and I'm going to deal with you anyway. If anybody asks why I accepted this film, I'll say I needed the money." Five thousand dollars wasn't so terribly much, but the economic conditions in Bulgaria were bad.

"I don't even have enough money to buy bulbs for the projectors in our theaters," he complained. "So I need the hard currency. But we'll only do a subtitled version. We only dub films for children."

I breathed a silent "Thank You" to the Lord, and told the president, "That will be fine."

A few weeks later I was back in the Soviet Union, for the third time in five months. I had five objectives:

- Expand the theater showings from two theaters to ten in the Republic of Georgia.

- See if it was possible to distribute a Gospel of Luke with follow-up Bible studies through the theaters. (Should we give them away, include them with the ticket and increase the price, or sell them?)

Ticket lines in Sofia, Bulgaria, stretched around the block after the film showings were announced on national television.

- Discern whether people attending a theater showing would fill out a comment card, telling us if they had received Jesus Christ through seeing the film or were interested in being in a Bible study.

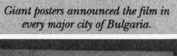

Giant posters announced the film in every major city of Bulgaria.

- Try to get a signed contract regarding the distribution of the Russian film nationwide.

- Produce a videotaped report on the Soviet Union that could be used to raise funds on television in America.

Is this what a missionary does? I wondered on my way to Moscow. It was my sixty-fifth flight of the year, and it was only May. For years I had spent the majority of my days talking to college students about knowing Christ personally. During my first year on the campus, more than seventy-five young men had prayed with me personally to receive Christ. I had talked with hundreds.

Now my personal evangelism was confined largely to airplanes, but I did have a role in helping others present the gospel through the "JESUS" film. Most of those activities were not so glamorous—just a lot of hard work and a lot of travel.

Travel means time away from home and family. Never could I do what I do without the understanding of a wonderful wife. It is because of her commitment to the Lord, to what we are doing together, and her sacrifices for our family that I have been able to be away so much.

I'm proud of our children and their hearts for the Lord. Sometimes it's hard to get on the plane. Someone once said, "No man ever died wishing he had spent more time at the office."

And so, the adventure of seeing the "JESUS" film spread to the corners of the globe has involved sacrifices on the part of Kathy, Jennifer, and Jonathan. I love them for being a part of the dream!

However, there are limits, especially when the children are in junior and senior high school. So Kathy and I have agreed that I would not be away more than a hundred nights a year unless she or the children were with me.

■ ■ ■ ■ ■

The early months of the opening of the Eastern Bloc countries were intoxicating. Our arrival back in Soviet Georgia launched another series of miraculous events. The reports after the first three months of film showings, with only two theater copies, indicated 542 showings to 149,000 people. Now we were expanding to ten theaters. Again the reception by government and film company officials was warm and the hospitality beyond belief.

A police escort took us on the four-hour drive across Georgia and delivered us to Kutaisi for the next premiere. On the way, we stopped at Stalin's birthplace. I walked through the house in which he was raised. His parents were simple working people who wanted him to become a priest, but his rejection of Christ and his persecution of the church ushered in an era of pain, godlessness, and tragedy unmatched in the history of the world.

The museum of Stalin is closed now. The history books no longer extol the virtues of this brutal killer. His statues have been taken down. But Jesus, whom he sought to eradicate from the Soviet conscience, still lives. And we were on the way to yet another showing of His story.

The Kutaisi premiere was another significant step forward in the strategy for the Soviet Union.

"I want to pass out comment cards tonight," I told Vaso, our theatrical coordinator in Georgia. "We want to find out what people think of the film."

"No problem," he said. "We'll announce before the film that we want people not to rush out immediately after the show but to remain long enough to fill out the cards."

I hoped they would stay. When I had tried to introduce the use of decision cards with the "JESUS" film showings in homes eighteen months earlier, everyone I talked to said it wouldn't work. But things were beginning to change. Now it was worth a try.

After the showing, everyone sat still. The 800-seat theater was packed, but we received only 255 cards. Many, we realized, didn't have a pencil or pen. Oh well, another thing to work on at a later showing.

I was eager to get the cards sorted and counted. The results were astounding. Of the 255 cards, 172 indicated that at the film's close they had prayed the prayer to receive Christ as their Savior and Lord. Fifteen people said they would like to study more about Jesus on their own. And 155 said they would like to be in a group Bible study to learn more about Jesus. The first steps in the follow-up process were being taken, and I was elated.

A few of the comments were translated for me the next day, and I found the honesty and expressions of the converts refreshing:

> Tonight I let Jesus Christ enter my life and deliver it. Unfortunately, we have been brought up in such a way that our souls have been torn out of us. We are soulless creatures. Through this film we can be restored to God...
>
> After seeing this film, I now believe in Jesus Christ...
>
> Tonight I received Christ as my Lord and Deliverer...
>
> This film has helped me to find the way to God...

I wished I could understand Georgian so I could read all the cards for myself.

We sold nearly 350 copies of the Gospel of Luke after the showings. But what we needed was a simple literature piece that we could afford to *give* to every person. Many organizations were printing Bibles. The need for simple follow-up literature was not being met. We would have to do some more planning.

Matt Prochaska and others went to work. To the Gospel of Luke they added an eight-page insert of color pictures taken from the film. They prepared background material—how and where the film was produced, and who is in it—much like you would find in a movie program.

They then added an article by Dr. Bright on the evidence for the resurrection of Jesus called "Who Is This Jesus?" and a copy of the *Four Spiritual Laws*. The final page was a tear-out form, so that we could gather the names and addresses of those who wanted more information on how to receive Christ.

When we had negotiated with the movie studios, we had promised a copy of the "script" of the film to every person who came. The studios were sure that this would increase attendance, and we rejoiced that there would be no opposition to our handing out the Gospel of Luke at every showing.

However, one major problem developed. All this was going to cost much more money than we could possibly raise. In fact, by July, most of our negotiation teams had returned with signed contracts. The schedule that lay ahead boggled our minds. God had answered our prayers for signed contracts with the movie studios in every country. But for each location, we had to estimate the following:

- How many theaters would show the film
- How many 35mm theatrical copies of the film would have to be produced
- How many people would watch the film so that we would know how many copies of the Gospel of Luke to print

We would have to translate the films and the Gospels into the proper languages. All these estimates had to be made within a few weeks—for countries that had never shown a Christian film in their history, and for countries that were still controlled by the Communist Party. Not an easy task.

Our initial planning sheet, showing some of the premiere dates that had been set, looked like this:

Premiere Date	City	Country (Republic)	Language	Gospels of Luke Needed	Films Needed
Sept. 21	Vilnius	Lithuania	Lithuanian	168,768	7
Oct. 6	Kishinev	Moldova	Moldovan	254,700	7
Oct. 19	Moscow	Russia	Russian	5,080,520	55
Oct. 21	Leningrad	Russia	Russian	400,000	5
Oct. 26	Kiev	Ukraine	Ukrainian	2,536,720	20
Nov. 1	Alma Ata	Kazakhstan	Kazakh	20,000	20
Nov. 3	Tashkent	Uzbekistan	Uzbek	20,000	5
Nov. 16	Dresden	E. Germany	German	417,600	10
Nov. 22	Prague	Czechoslovakia	Czech	1,019,960	24
Nov. 23	Bratislava	Czechoslovakia	Slovak	235,200	16
Dec. 7	Tallinn	Estonia	Estonian	120,800	4
Dec. 7	Sofia	Bulgaria	Bulgarian	208,000	5
Dec. 12	Budapest	Hungary	Hungarian	207,240	15
Dec. 14	Riga	Latvia	Latvian	140,800	6
Dec. 14	Bucharest	Romania	Romanian	1,202,400	15
			TOTAL:	12,032,708	214

We were in big trouble. There were not nearly enough funds. Stephen Freed, who was giving major leadership to the project, walked into my office with a sheaf of papers.

"Do you know how much it will cost to roll this out everywhere like we are talking about?" he asked.

"Several million dollars or more, I'm sure," I said.

"I'm figuring a little over four million, counting production, shipping and storage of the Gospels of Luke, the premieres, plus what we owe the studios in every country on our contracts." He pushed his calculations across the desk so that I could see them in black and white.

"We've got our necks out pretty far on some of these commitments," he noted. "It's not going to be easy to get out of them if we have to cancel."

"Well, let's pray that the Lord brings in the funds," I responded. We prayed again for God to supply the resources. Although it was a project far beyond us, we believed together that the Lord had supernaturally opened the door, and that He would supernaturally supply the funds.

However, we would only go forward as the money became available. If we didn't have the funds, we would make only one copy of the film for each language. We would print only enough copies of the Gospels of Luke for the opening night, and so on. I didn't want to be raising funds for a deficit. I was sure the Lord could bring the money in ahead of time if He wanted us to go forward.

He did.

The friends and foundations who provided the funds were a very great encouragement to me personally. One day they will receive their reward from the Heavenly Father. In the meantime, I can only say thank you to them for their confidence and trust in us—that we would use the money strategically and carefully for the cause of His kingdom. I am so very grateful!

A few weeks later the premieres started, and we were in high gear!

CHAPTER 6

Opening Night
in Moscow

Premiere week in Moscow opened with a flurry of last-minute preparations. The first of sixty Americans who would be special guests boarded planes for Moscow. The offices erupted into a frenzy of activity as we attempted to prepare all the materials we would need in the next few days. During that time, we would hold premieres in three cities, meet with 1,300 pastors in three two-hour training sessions, and conduct a variety of outreaches to business and government leaders.

The "to-do" list seemed endless: Call Pan Am and tell them we have forty-three extra pieces of luggage—we are 3,600 pounds overweight. Buy steel containers for the ten 35mm films to protect them during shipping, and repack them firmly for the theaters. Buy two carry-on bags and hand carry the Moscow premiere copy of the film in case the luggage is lost. Pack three hundred 8×10 pictures of Jesus to be used as special gifts for premiere guests. Pack 1,250 videocassettes in six languages for delivery to pastors and government officials. Pick up the training material for pastors at the printer. Insert a hundred theatrical posters into tubes for shipping. Get the airway bill numbers for thirty-nine boxes of training material already shipped by DHL, an international delivery service. Buy gifts for film company officials for a presentation at the premiere banquet. Pack 10,000 Russian *Four Spiritual Laws* booklets for distribution by guests during the trip. Rent a truck to take boxes to the airport. Find out why 3,500 Russian Gospels of Luke had not arrived. And on and on.

At 4:30 p.m. a truck pulled in with the Gospels of Luke. These 88-page booklets were a big part of the strategy. The "opinion card" contained in the back would allow us to find out who had indicated decisions to receive Christ at these premieres.

By 9 p.m. everything was ready, and our staff headed home to pack their own suitcases. I stopped by the grocery store for more breakfast bars. Sometimes the food was not so plentiful in the Soviet hotels, unless you want bread and tea for every meal.

Wednesday and Thursday sped by in Moscow. The special guests toured the city, joined a prayer service at the Moscow Central Baptist Church, and talked about Jesus with people on the streets. A visit to the New Life Training Center permitted opportunities to meet new believers who had become Christians through seeing the "JESUS" film, and who were now involved in study groups to grow in their faith.

I spent most of my days making sure the last-minute arrangements for the program were completed and that each person who would speak was briefed. I also prepared for the first meeting with Juli Gusman, director of Dom Kino, the House of Filmmakers, where the premiere would be held.

"The response for tickets for this film is absolutely fantastic," he bubbled. "We are sold out! The 1,200 seats in the main arena are all gone. We have opened our small hall which seats six hundred for a simultaneous showing, and all of those seats are filled. Now people are calling and becoming very angry because they can't get tickets. So we are scheduling a third showing tomorrow at noon to try to handle the demand."

He paused and smiled, "Who would have ever dreamed that people in this country would be fighting over tickets to a film on the life of Jesus?"

I sat in the empty theater watching the film crews set up their cameras and arrange the extra lights. It was a beautiful setting. The wood floor on the expansive stage had been polished to a brilliant sheen, and a new plush velvet curtain had just been hung. But there was something else.

On the left side of the stage on the wall that angled out slightly toward the audience, a twelve-foot, velvet-covered, round placard had been hung. On the placard in beautiful gold letters was the word *Jesus*. An identical placard containing Cyrillic lettering hung on the other side.

"What does that sign say?" I asked Juli, pointing to the one on the right of the stage.

"Those are the same words you asked to be placed on the posters," he said. " 'I am the resurrection and the life; he that believes in Me shall never die.' Do you like it?"

I choked back tears. "It's wonderful."

More than a year before, we discovered that the film companies in each country and republic wanted to make their own posters. Ambitious studio people would print them to sell to make a little money on the side. Rather than try to control all of this, which was impossible anyway, we simply wrote a special clause into all the contracts: "Any posters produced, whether for sale or for advertising, must contain this quote from Jesus: 'I am the resurrection and the life...' "

In a few minutes the doors would open. Some of the most influential people in all the Soviet Union would gather here in the House of Filmmakers. And for the next three hours they would be looking at our Lord's name and His wonderful promise: "He that believes in Me shall never die!"

The theater officials arrived to take me to the pre-premiere VIP reception.

"Give me just a minute," I said. "I'll be right there."

In that minute I just said, "Thank You, Lord, for doing all of this. Thank You for opening the doors. Thank You for letting me

The Moscow premiere in the House of Filmmakers.

see some of Your miracles. Now Lord, give us Your wisdom to
know what to say as we speak tonight before the film is shown.
Amen."

The reception room was jammed. The introductions came
fast from Juli.

"Paul, meet the Minister of Culture..."

"Say hello to the Deputy Minister of Russia..."

"Here is the greatest director in Soviet theater..."   .

"Paul, meet Olga Polykovskaya from the Ministry of Education..."

And so it went as Communist Party officials and leaders from
the Moscow city government, the Russian Republic, and the
Soviet Union arrived. Five members of the Supreme Soviet were
there, as well as seven of nine ministers of the Russian Republic
government.

The evening was part of our long-term strategy. We used the
occasion of the premiere to invite the top political, religious, and
social leaders to see the film. Perhaps they would come out of
curiosity, or because it was the first Western film dubbed in their
language, or just because the Spirit of God drew them in an
unexplainable, supernatural way.

The strategy was to start with the top leadership of the country
and ask those leaders who saw the film to open doors for further
showings to all parts of society. Would it work in the Soviet Union?
Would they respond to the film? We would know in a few hours.

Then it was time to go from the reception to the main hall.
Juli led the way to the main lobby. Ushers tore the corners from
our tickets to make sure we would not try to take more than one
copy of the Gospel of Luke. Closed-circuit television sets spaced
every fifty feet throughout the lobby showed films of the recent
worship service held inside the Kremlin. During the "JESUS" film
showing, it would be playing on these television sets as well, for
the benefit of the ushers and others unable to get in.

The Russian Orthodox Church had set up displays of religious
art in the foyers, and souvenir stands were selling special "JESUS"
posters produced for the film.

Everywhere we looked, television film crews were interviewing
the crowd and the celebrities. All three Soviet national channels
took part, along with two networks of Soviet radio, film crews from

five other countries, reporters and photographers from *Pravda* and *Isvestia,* and scores of magazine reporters and critics.

Two thousand guests, dressed in their finery, added to the electric atmosphere of the milling crowd. The twinkling lights of the brilliant lobbies were outshone only by the sweep of the TV cameras as reporters conducted interviews in every corner. The excited chatter of the entering crowd eventually drowned out the beautiful sounds of the orchestral chamber group. And then it was time to begin.

We filed on stage to very warm applause. Juli Gusman, director of Dom Kino, presided. In glowing words, he welcomed the crowd to the 27th season of special film presentations. And he told about the decision to open their season with quite an unusual film.

For Juli, it was a calculated risk. Not everyone would be glad it was a religious film. It was possible to lose face, to lose respect, even to be replaced in his job. Though things were changing fast in the Soviet Union, position still equaled power. And power made possible better apartments, better stores to shop in, travel abroad, and so on.

What Juli personally thought about Jesus was difficult to determine. As with most other studio directors, he had begun this project simply as a business arrangement. He was not signing up to be a missionary to bring Jesus to the Soviet Union. Yet, somehow, that was what he was doing. And I got the feeling that he hoped the speeches given by me, Dr. Bright, and General Jackson would not embarrass him.

We would not. The purpose here was only to open the doors. Let the film speak for itself. No need to preach.

Then the first speaker, the president of the Filmmakers Union, was introduced. He wore an open-necked yellow shirt and a natty sport coat. No tie. When did you ever see a movie director in a tie?

His words were amazing. After the perfunctory greeting, he said, "I understand that Jesus once said, 'Where two or three are gathered together in My name, I am in the midst of them.' So Jesus will be here with us tonight as we watch this film." Pretty strong stuff from a Communist Party member. I rejoiced.

Then I was introduced. "I want you to meet the man who has supervised the translation of this film into 174 languages and

directed the distribution into 166 countries. He is the director of
The JESUS Film Project from California in the United States, Paul
Eshleman."

I had been praying about what to say. It seemed best to give
the background of the film. That would be of primary interest to
the filmwatchers attending.

"Tonight you will see a very special motion picture," I began.
"Any filmmaker would, of course, be a little nervous to present his
film before an audience such as this. What you will view on the
screen is very simply and straightforwardly presented. Many of
you would have other ideas for its visual interpretation.

"But the impact of this film is not in its cinematography, or its
acting, or its directing. The impact is in the words—the words of
Jesus."

The film, I told the audience, was produced by John Heyman,
winner of an award at the Cannes Film Festival. "It was filmed in
Israel, as close as possible to where the actual events took place
two thousand years ago." I continued my usual introduction of
the film, talking about its accuracy and the years of research
involved in the production, and then finished with a progress
report on its distribution.

"According to Jack Valenti, president of the Motion Picture
Association of America, 'JESUS' is the most translated film in
history. It already has been seen by 425 million people, and by
next spring it will be available in twenty different languages for
the Soviet Union. I want to offer my congratulations to Gorky
Film Studios for their very fine dubbing.

"And I want to thank Juli Gusman, Alex Bermont, and the
Mirage Organization, who are heading the theatrical distribution.

"One of the directors of Warner Brothers Pictures, who distributed the film in two thousand movie theaters in North America, was asked what he thought of the film. He replied, 'The
"JESUS" film is two hours of peace in a world full of chaos.' I hope
this film will help bring peace to your life. And I hope you enjoy
the picture. Thank you!"

The applause was warm. My speech was not spectacular, but it
needed to be short because of the translation.

In rapid-fire order, the other speakers were introduced and
came to the microphone. The Soviet side was represented by the

deputy prime minister of Russia, perhaps the number three man behind Boris Yeltsin in the powerful republic.

Then Juli introduced the general. "This film premiere is another occasion for the building of friendship and ties between the United States and the USSR," he noted. "For years in the past, our governments have been locked in a so-called Cold War. Tonight, I want you to meet a warrior who is here in the cause of peace. He is Major General John Jackson of the United States Air Force. Welcome, General!"

As in the Georgian premiere, the appearance of an American general caused a ripple of comments to run through the crowd. But they applauded enthusiastically when he told of the admirals and generals in the Pentagon who meet weekly to pray for peace.

I sat on the stage looking out at the beautifully decorated theater with its lush, red carpeting and Dolby stereo sound. More than seventy American guests filled our section. Another area was filled with church leaders, some from the All-Union Council of Baptists (the umbrella group of most Protestant churches), and others dressed in the long, black robes of the Orthodox Church. This historic occasion would be impressed indelibly on every mind.

Juli paused to make a special presentation.

"Before I introduce the next person to bring greetings, I want you to meet some very special people. All of us involved in the theater and filmmaking know the importance of having financial backing. The finances for the production of this film, six million dollars, were provided by Mr. Bunker Hunt and his wife, Caroline. They are seated here in the front. Will you please stand, Mr. and Mrs. Hunt, so we can recognize you?"

One of the young women from the premiere staff presented them with bouquets of flowers.

A short speech by the minister of culture followed, and then Juli introduced Dr. Bright.

"Our last American guest to speak is Dr. Bill Bright. He is a writer, an educator, and a Christian leader. He is the president of the international organization New Life that has branches in 135 countries. He is the one who had the idea for this film on the life of Jesus. His organization hopes to make the film available to every country in the world."

Dr. Bill Bright, founder of Campus Crusade for Christ (known in Eurasia as New Life), had the original vision to produce a film on Christ's life.

Bill gave warm greetings and told of his love and prayers for the Russian people for more than forty years. His words were poignant, and enthusiastically received.

It was now time to start the film. I asked Juli if he would prepare the group to give us their opinions. He did an excellent job.

"Tonight as you came in," he said, "you received a copy of the Gospel of Luke. This is the portion of the Bible from which the script of this film has been taken. On the last page of this booklet you will find a form on which you can write what you think about the film. The producers would like to know.

"Would you be so kind as to carefully tear out the last page of this very nice booklet right now." He paused until they started tearing them out, then continued, "This will be a reminder to you. Then after the film is over, please write your opinion. You can place the form in one of the boxes by the doors as you leave the theater. Thank you very much."

We left the stage quickly and were escorted to our seats as the film started. We began to watch and pray. This was the first public showing of the new Russian dubbing. How would the people respond? About halfway through, two of them got up and walked out. My heart fell. In a few moments, another couple left, then two women.

I started counting. Soon ten had left; then two came back. Maybe it was just a trip to the restroom.

I worried. I had told the group of sixty Americans how much the Soviet people liked the film. I had told them of the standing ovation in Georgia. Now people were walking out and I felt responsible.

It was again time to pray. "Lord, this is Your film showing. Our purpose is to lift up Jesus. It's all up to You. We've been faithful to get the film and the people here. But You have to speak to them."

Two or three more people left, but the majority were transfixed, their eyes glued to the screen.

The film reached its last five minutes, the explanation of the gospel. This was the prayer of invitation to receive Christ. These people were the sophisticated elite of the Soviet cinema. What would happen?

Nobody moved. When the film was over, it received quiet, respectful applause. No great ovation as in Georgia.

Still worried, I began to ask people what they thought. Then, surprised, I noticed that many had tears in their eyes.

An actress handed me her response sheet and I asked her what she thought.

"It was marvelous! Words can't describe how I feel tonight," she gushed. "I am going home a better person than when I came."

"Did you pray the prayer at the end of the film to invite Jesus to be your Savior and Lord?" I probed.

"Of course," she said. There was a slight note of disdain in her voice, as if it was inconceivable that someone would not want to accept Christ.

"Why wasn't the applause louder?" I asked.

She answered somewhat impatiently, "You don't know Russians, do you? You don't play drums after a prayer. These people are thinking thoughts they have never thought before. They are not going to be clapping while they are thinking about God. Don't you understand? We have never had a film like this, a film about God. I am so filled up. I cannot tell you how I am feeling. This has been a wonderful night."

And then people everywhere were talking about the impact of the film. We were ushered to the premiere banquet in the Dom Kino Restaurant for a time of celebration—toasts, speeches, and introductions. There were chairs, but no one sat.

Through the din, I talked with reporters and celebrities. An Orthodox archpriest was warm and responsive.

"This is a wonderful gift you have brought us," he enthused. "This film is like a missionary. Many atheists will never come to our churches, but we can take the film to meeting halls and other secular places, and help bring people to God."

He introduced us to the bishop assisting Patriarch Alexi.

"How many dioceses are there in the USSR?" I asked.

"About a hundred," he replied.

"As soon as the theater showings are completed we would like to give a copy of the film to every diocese," I offered.

"That would be wonderful," he beamed. "We must have a meeting with the Patriarch."

Then I met the actor who had been the Russian voice of Jesus. He was 33. *Just about the right age,* I thought.

"You did a wonderful job," I complimented.

"This was a very meaningful film for us," he replied slowly. "Thank you for giving us the opportunity."

So many people had worked together to make this night possible. One couple had financed the film. Another had paid for the Russian translation. A foundation had given the Gospels of Luke and paid for the film copies. A Russian film studio had done the dubbing of a script translated by workers from a Christian mission in the USSR. An Azerbaijan Jew had organized the premiere, and a Russian company was setting up the theater showings. And everywhere, people prayed.

At 1:30 a.m., I caught the last car to the hotel with the U.S. television crew. What an unforgettable night. Tomorrow we would get the responses from the opinion sheets and find out the results of all the conversations that had been held by others in our group.

For tonight, it was enough to say, "Thank You, dear Father, for letting our eyes witness Your divine touch in the Moscow theater. Amen."

CHAPTER 7

A New Beginning for Albania

In 1967 Albania had declared itself the first atheistic country in the world. It had closed the doors of all of its churches, and exiled, imprisoned, or killed its pastors and priests. While people went without food, the dictator, Enver Hoxha, built monuments to himself. But he continued persecuting anyone who dared to try anything religious. He ordered crosses to be cut off tombstones so every remembrance of Jesus would be wiped out. Finally, he started arresting anyone who criticized anything he did.

Was it possible to take the film to Albania? The entire Eastern Bloc had now opened to the gospel—but not Albania. It had been one of the countries most closed to Christianity. Still locked in a totalitarian system, the country had not yet broken through to democracy. Hoxha was dead, but the Communists were still in power. With the fall of Ceaucescu in Romania, Albanians began to hope that things might change for them.

As we made inquiries about visas and about what was going on in the country, we began to hear unbelievable stories. For example, one man had been arrested more than thirty years ago just for commenting that he didn't think one of Hoxha's decisions was good. While in the prison camp, he had grown a little garden to feed himself. When he was released just before we got there, he found the economy so bad and conditions so bleak, he just went back to the prison. At least there he had a little food to eat, and he really had no place to go after all those years, anyway.

Six months after the fall of Romania, a visa was finally granted to Stephen Freed in our office to go into Albania for the negotiations. We were all praying for his trip when word came that the

77

Albania Film Company had agreed to allow the distribution of the film. We were overjoyed.

We decided to begin with the Albanian version that we had dubbed for the Albanian speakers in nearby Yugoslavia.

On a cold December morning I flew out of Zurich, Switzerland, with a group of forty staff members and interested laymen, bound for Albania. It was an answer to years of prayers by many people who refused to give up on the people of Albania even though the country was so tightly closed for so long.

As I stepped into the plane, it seemed that God started unleashing an avalanche of His Spirit. What happened in the next three days could only have been by the hand of God.

I had been seated in the plane for just a few minutes when one of the members of our group came up to my seat to talk. "I'm sitting next to the mayor of the second largest city in Albania," he said. "He is a member of the new democratic political party and his group has been visiting other countries trying to understand what a democracy is really like. He would like to meet you."

I stepped to the back, and we talked about the upcoming premiere of the "JESUS" film in Tirana. I invited him to attend. The flight attendant was trying to serve, so I sat down in the empty seat next to him and we continued to talk. He was incredibly curious about spiritual things. He introduced me to a man who had just gotten out of prison. He had served more than ten years in a detention camp simply for making a negative statement about Hoxha.

"I think this is a good time for you to bring your film to Albania," the mayor began. "We have not been permitted to study religion for twenty-four years, and there is much interest now. I myself am Muslim."

"All of us come from some kind of religious tradition," I said. "But at some point in our development, we have to decide for ourselves if we believe what we have been told all of our lives. We decide whether we will follow the religion of our parents or not."

I told him I had been raised in a Christian home but had made my own decision to believe in Jesus Christ as the way to God after really understanding what the issues were. Then I showed him the *Four Spiritual Laws* booklet.

"The Bible is a very big book," I commented, "but this pamphlet helps to point out the key information you need to know to begin. Would you like to see it?"

"Certainly."

"Okay, I'll just read it through with you."

When I finished reading the first Law, he said, "I like that Law. It is nice to think about having a plan for your life."

By the time we got to the second Law, he was reading the booklet out loud to me. He was forty-eight years old and in the last few years had taught himself to speak English by watching American TV programs on Italian television and looking up the words in a dictionary.

We looked at the definition of sin—active rebellion or passive indifference to God. "I'm not rebellious," he said. "I think that I have just been indifferent because of our system."

We talked about the fact that Jesus was the only religious leader who ever claimed to be able to forgive sins. That was why it was so important to consider His claims. The mayor agreed. We read John 1:12:

As many as received Him, to them He gave the right to become children of God, even to those who believe in His Name (NASB).

"I understand," he nodded. "If I receive Jesus as the payment for my sin, then I will become a son of God." We read on. We talked about the meaning of grace, works, faith, and what we are saved from. It was important that we not get into a debate on which religious philosophy was best or which system of thought gives you the best lifestyle. We talked about how one can be forgiven and be sure of eternal life with God. Finally, we arrived at Revelation 3:20:

Behold, I stand at the door and knock; if anyone hears My voice and opens the door, I will come in to him (NASB).

"What is that door to?" I asked him.

"I suppose to myself, my soul," he responded.

"And what does Jesus say He will do if we open the door?"

"He says He will come in," he responded quickly.

"Now," I said, "let me show you how you can open the door and invite Jesus to come in." We read the prayer at the back of the booklet and I explained that it was not the words that were important, but the attitude of his heart. He seemed so ready. All around us his friends were leaning over trying to listen to the conversation. He told them he would tell them all about it later and we promised to give each of them a Gospel of Luke booklet as soon as we arrived and picked up our baggage. So I said, "Would you like to read this prayer and invite Jesus to be your personal Savior?"

"I can read this prayer, of course," he replied. "But, according to what you have told me, I must also sincerely believe the words. I am not sure that I am ready to make this invitation yet."

At first I was disappointed. There seemed nothing in particular holding him back. But who responds to the message is none of my business. Jesus has sent me out as a witness, not a convincer. I thought about the admonition in our class on personal evangelism: "Successful witnessing is taking the initiative to share Christ in the power of the Holy Spirit, and leaving the results to God." He understood, and that was the issue. And Muslims are interested in the message of Jesus. It would be evident the next morning.

At nine o'clock I walked into an English class at the University of Tirana. The best and the brightest in Albania were selected to go to this school, which prepared future translators for government and business. If Albania was to get back in touch with the world, it would need many interpreters, and they would need to be accurate.

I had barely finished introducing our team of three when a dark-haired girl in the first row raised her hand. "I was wondering if you could tell us how we can talk to God. We don't know how to talk to God."

"We call talking to God *prayer*," I answered. "At the end of my talk today I will show you how you can talk to God. I will pray out loud, phrase by phrase, and you can say the words silently to God if you would like."

There was a sudden buzzing in the class as they turned to whisper to each other. It was almost as if they were saying, "We're going to talk to God today. We're going to talk to God!"

Tamara, a young staff member from Poland, told her story of coming to faith from a background of atheism. The students all related well to her situation. That's where they all were. It's what they all had been taught. They had never known anything else.

Evaleen Harris gave her testimony, and then I was on. I spoke slowly. I explained each term. These were second-year English students, but for most of them it was the first time they had ever spoken with an American in person.

At the end of my talk, I said I would now give them a chance to receive Christ. The girl in the first row said that all of her relatives were Muslim. "It doesn't matter what your background is," I said. "When you come to the age of university students, whether you are in America or Albania, you have to make up your own mind whether you will follow what your parents believe, or whether you will investigate on your own.

"You will remember that I said earlier that we would close the session by talking to God. There are many ways to pray. Some people bow their heads to the ground. Others kneel. In our country it is the custom to bow your head out of reverence for the God who created the world. And we close our eyes so that we are not distracted and are able to think only of God. I will pray first, phrase by phrase. If you would like to accept Jesus as the payment for your sins, you may say these same words to God, silently where you sit."

We prayed. My eyes were closed, but it seemed to me that I could hear the quiet whisper of some of the students repeating the prayer after me. We passed out some cards to get their comments and questions.

One student wrote, "I am Muslim, but somehow I prefer to place my faith in Jesus. I don't know why. It is a wonder that I cannot explain."

Another card said, "No one in my whole life has told me how to know God. Please help me!" At the top of the card the box was checked that indicated she had prayed with me to receive Christ. It was Anilla, the girl in the first row.

She stopped to talk as she was leaving. "Did you pray that prayer with me at the end?" I asked.

She looked embarrassed. "Well, yes, I did say the prayer. But once I opened my eyes because I thought the prayer was over."

"It's okay," I smiled. "God hears you whether your eyes are open or closed." Her innocence was refreshing. She wanted so desperately to know God. And she wanted to do it in the right way, whatever that was.

I began to ask her the questions I have asked many others who have made their decisions to receive Christ.

"Did you ask Jesus to come into your life and forgive your sins?"

"Yes."

"Then where is Jesus now in relation to you?"

She pointed to her heart.

"Now let me show you one other verse."

We read 1 John 5:12: "He who has the Son has the life; he who does not have the Son of God does not have the life" (NASB).

I asked, "Do you have the Son now in your life?"

"Yes."

"Then what kind of life do you have?"

"Eternal life," she beamed.

"When does it end?" I asked.

"Never."

"And when did it begin for you?"

"Just a few moments ago." She understood. The first time she heard the Good News, she responded. How many in Albania were just like her? We would see in the days ahead.

A few hours later it was time for the theatrical premiere. Congressman Bob McEwen and his wife, Liz, had arrived and we were soon on our way to the Palace of Congresses. The Albania Film Company, once the propaganda tool of the now-dead Communist dictator, had been preparing for this event for weeks. As we spoke to people in the city, we discovered most of them were aware of the film's coming. Small clips of it had been shown on television every night during the last week, and eight or ten newspaper articles about it had been run even before it opened.

As we drove up to the elegant palace, I reflected on the desperate need in Albania. The entire cabinet had resigned the day before we arrived. New elections were being planned, but there was great unrest. Strikes were commonplace. The electricity was on only sporadically. Most buildings had no heat. I wore my overcoat most of the time inside the hotel because the rooms were so cold.

And everywhere, wood fires and their smoke filled the streets. People huddled around the fires for warmth. Every tree on the road leading in from the airport had been cut down for firewood. Beleaguered, stooped men in dirty coveralls chopped away at the tree stumps trying to coax out a few more wood chips for their fires. Unemployment was rampant. A law allowing people to draw 80 percent of their salary without working had resulted in mobs of people wandering the streets. Nothing to buy. No work, and not much food. Thousands homeless. Three or four families crammed into one small decaying flat. The United Nations had just classified this bleak, gray land as a "developing country."

The Palace of Congresses stood in marked contrast to the rest of the country. Built by Hoxha for the Communist Party congresses, it boasted two thousand seats, marble floors, and crystal chandeliers.

The film community and political leaders packed the pre-premiere reception. Word came that the square in front of the building was jammed with people trying to get in. More than a thousand had to be turned away. The ministers of culture and education, slated to give opening remarks, couldn't get through the crowd, and we had to start without them.

That night was awesome. Congressman McEwen talked about the need to build a new Albania on the teachings of Jesus, and I gave some background on the production of the film.

Then we had the response from the director of the film studio. His words were powerful. "We are gathered together tonight for the first film showing ever to be held in this building. We are showing the film, 'JESUS.' And tonight Jesus will be speaking Albanian. This building was erected as the temple of communism, but for the next two hours I declare it to be the temple of Jesus."

I wiped the tears out of my eyes. Who would have believed this could take place in Albania, the most atheistic country in the world?

A warm, enthusiastic applause erupted at the end of the showing. I went back to the stage to ask the people to tear the comment cards out of the back of the Gospel of Luke booklets that they had been given. All over the auditorium people were already quietly writing.

More than eight hundred cards were returned. On these, five hundred and fifty indicated that they had received Christ, and more than four hundred wanted to study the Bible. By the end of the three days, nearly eight hundred Albanians had expressed a desire to receive the Lord.

At the close of the premiere, I had announced an open meeting the next afternoon for those who wanted to know more about Jesus. More than four hundred people came that next day. I explained that our group was made up of members of three new churches that had just started in the city.

"Since many of you have never been in a church before," I began, "I want to tell you a little bit about what a church is like. There are many different kinds of churches. They can be held in any kind of building—some churches have big buildings; others are small and very simple."

I paused to phrase my explanation in gentle but accurate terms. "Different churches are started because people have different ideas about how to best worship the Lord. Anyone can go to a church whether he or she is a believer in Jesus or not. Jesus never turned anyone away, so a faithful Christian church always welcomes those who seek to know the truth."

I looked over the expectant faces. Everyone seemed to be listening intently. "Usually four or five things happen in a church meeting. We have a time to talk to God. As you know, that is called prayer. We read from the Bible so we can know how God wants us to live. We learn about what the Scriptures mean and we study the words of Jesus.

"In addition, we usually sing songs of praise to God," I announced. "Today some people from one of the new churches here in Tirana will lead us in these songs of worship. It is not a concert. You can join in the singing as well."

Bud Hinkson spoke on how Jesus fulfilled the prophecies made hundreds of years before. When he gave the invitation to receive Christ, nearly two hundred responded.

The following day brought meetings with members of Parliament and the heads of the four political parties, and a luncheon with the prime minister. He told us that he was very impressed with the film, and that he was reading the Gospel of Luke to his son and recalling the scenes they had seen at the premiere. I spent most of the meal sharing my testimony with the head of the Socialist Party in Parliament. I presented New Testaments to all the leaders at the luncheon—all but one came from Muslim backgrounds. Each person I talked with responded positively to the film.

One man summed up his impressions of the film by saying, "You can see what has happened to this country as a result of living without God. You have brought us Jesus, and a new beginning!"

The Communist stranglehold on Eastern Europe was starting to collapse and millions were hearing the gospel. But there were other places in other countries where people hadn't heard the message yet, not because of communism but because no one had gone to them. Unreached groups of people could be found in so many remote spots of the world—people like the rebels fighting in El Salvador, the mountain people of Nepal, the Kurds in Iraq, and the Fulanis of Nigeria...

CHAPTER 8

To the Ends of the Earth

S ome months later after the Albanian premiere, as our jeep bumped along the dusty, gravel road in northern Nigeria, I thought, *How desperately the people of this African country also need to feel the supernatural touch of Jesus.* His touch could reach down into a discouraged, defeated heart and give great hope. Hope for this life, but more importantly, hope for an unending life with the Creator.

Conditions were tense here. Dr. Timothy Gyuse, heading all showings of the "JESUS" film in West Africa, gave us the briefing.

"We're glad you've come, Paul, but this is a dangerous time here. Our entire area is now under martial law," he explained. "During the last three days we have been on the edge of revolution. Muslim radicals have been on a killing and burning spree through the northern states of our country, burning Christian churches and killing pastors. They want to make Nigeria a fundamentalist Muslim state and introduce Sharia law."

I grimaced. I remembered the situation in Sudan. Sharia law calls for a thief to have his hands cut off. If he is caught breaking into a home, one of his legs is cut off as well. The reports from Sudan were saying that since the introduction of Sharia law in that country, the murder rate had gone up alarmingly. Thieves who were surprised in the middle of a burglary would immediately kill whoever saw them rather than risk being identified and having one of their arms or legs amputated.

"What exactly has happened?" I inquired.

"So far, things here in Jos have been pretty quiet," he replied. "But our brothers in Kaduna and Kano have not been so fortunate." One pastor, he explained, was set on fire, and he burned to death in front of his congregation. The son of another pastor was knifed in the stomach when he tried to protect the church from being burned. "In all, they have burned more than a hundred churches to the ground in the last three days. Now there is a dusk-to-dawn curfew."

I saw the sadness in his eyes and heard the tremble in his voice. Some of those whose churches had been burned had been his friends. But, suddenly, he brightened.

"You know, though," he smiled, "this past Sunday, those churches held their services anyway. The people stood among the ashes and praised the living God and asked Him to forgive the ones who had burned down their churches. Their response has been so forgiving that pictures of these praise services have been carried on national television. It has been a wonderful testimony for the church in this country."

I thought, *Jesus Christ will build His church, and the gates of hell will not prevail against it.*

Tim continued his briefing. "Tonight we are going to have the premiere showing of the 'JESUS' film for the Fulanis. This tribe of Muslim nomadic herdsmen is one of the least-reached groups of people in the whole world. There are more than eleven million of them. Fulanis speak a language called Fulfulde, and tonight will be the first showing of the film in that language.

"As you know," Tim explained, "there is a curfew now. But the people in this area have been waiting more than a year to see this film, and they don't want to wait one day longer. We will take you out to the backcountry, at least twenty miles from a paved road, so I don't believe we will have any problems."

I looked over at my friend Jim Blankemeyer as we bounced along in the jeep. He was a manufacturer by trade, but his passion was helping people everywhere to hear the message of Christ. We were not in Africa by accident. We had come as a team for this very purpose, to help committed national leaders like Tim and his staff show this life-changing film "JESUS" to his whole country. For one tribe, the Fulanis, it would begin tonight.

What was the secret of the great acceptance of the film? Why such an enormous response?

Perhaps because it was simply the Scriptures brought to life on the motion picture screen. The Lord says that His Word will not return void when it is given out. This was the Fulanis' experience. Those who watched sat captivated by what they saw.

In the film, they see Jesus living as simply as they. One woman in India said, "When I saw Jesus walking around in the film, He never carried a suitcase. He was poor like me, and I knew He could understand my problems."

Most of the people who watched the film are still living physically in a first-century culture. They still fished or farmed for a living, so they readily identified with Jesus.

The showings in the Soviet Union had been in theaters. But as the "JESUS" film began to spread across the world, the venues changed dramatically. In media-sophisticated areas, the method was television, videocassette, or theatrical release. But in the rural areas of the world, the film would be shown by 16mm projector.

Tonight that would take place among the Fulanis. First, a generator would be started up to provide electricity. Then the screen would be set up. And as darkness fell, hundreds of men, women, and children would come out of the bush to see the story of God's Son, the one true God who created the world.

Finally we arrived at the site.

"This is it," Tim announced. "Let's get set up."

It was a classic showing, and Tim's men were well trained. The screen frame was quickly assembled and the white sailcloth attached to it. A level ground area was located and the legs were then attached to the screen to lift it six feet above the heads of the crowd. This would allow many more to see, and keep hands and heads out of the picture. And because the screen was free-standing in the middle of the field, people could watch the picture from either side. I don't know how this works, but it does, and more people can see the film.

A slender young man wearing a Kansas State T-shirt placed the generator behind a nearby shed to muffle the sound and ran the power cord to the projector being set up. One of the big businesses in Africa is the importation of used clothing, so it's not unusual to see someone with a T-shirt from Kansas State, Disneyland, or some other place.

A film team worker threads the 16mm projector.

Loudspeakers were attached to the screen frame and the film was threaded onto the projector. A string of light bulbs ran from the top of the screen to the branch of one of the few trees nearby. These bulbs would provide light for the personal counseling that would take place after the showing.

When it was time to begin, one of the local men who spoke Fulfulde took the microphone. "Tonight, you will have a chance to see the first film ever translated into the Fulfulde language," he began. "Please come in a little closer and sit down. We will begin in a few moments.

"This film is the story of the prophet Jesus, spoken of in the Koran. It has been translated into more languages than any other film in history. People in every country of the world are interested

A giant forty-foot screen is set up to accommodate the 20,000 people meeting in an African stadium.

in seeing this film because it tells the story of the Son of the God who created the world.

"The film has four reels and lasts two hours. We will stop after each reel to change it. The lights will come on then, so do not be surprised. After the film ends, we would like to get your opinions on it, so we will be speaking to you again at that time. Now, here is the film called 'JESUS.'"

Jim and I searched for a log to sit on. It was a warm African night with sparkling stars and just enough of a breeze to keep the mosquitos away. I had taken my malaria pills, but you could never be absolutely sure. I'd talked to enough of the "JESUS" film team workers in that part of the world to know that the U.S. doctors didn't always know the best doses to prevent certain kinds of malaria.

That afternoon I had talked with one of the young women who was in Nigeria helping train the workers. They were learning to follow up those who became believers in Christ as a result of seeing the film. She had malaria. She was weak, but had no thoughts of going home.

"I'll be all right in a few weeks," she sighed. "You just feel so drained all the time. And it tends to come back over and over."

I marveled at her dedication.

I pulled my wandering mind back to the film showing before me. When it started, fewer than a hundred people were watching.

"Is there a village around here somewhere?" I had asked a film worker.

"No, these Fulanis are wanderers," he replied. "They are moving their cattle now, so we have just come to this new land where they are grazing their herds. They will pass the word about this showing and people will come soon."

He was right. There were now more than 250 watching the film.

Most of the crowd sat quietly in the dust, children in the front near the screen with their mothers behind them. And gradually the men, even the old chiefs, gathered around the back in the shadows.

Many of these, I realized, had never seen a film before. At my request, the interpreter asked the crowd how many had never seen a film. Nearly three-fourths of them raised their hands.

When asked how many had never seen an electric light, more than half raised their hands.

In those situations, we know we will have to stay for several days because people are so overwhelmed initially by the technology. In fact, the first time they see a "head shot" of a character, the crowd begins to buzz. You can hear them talking among themselves:

"Look at that poor man. He has no body."

"I wonder how he gets around."

"Someone must carry him in a bag."

As I looked at the picture on the screen this night, I wondered at its clarity. We had brought some new copies from the laboratory with us and this was one of them. It was as clear and beautiful as any I had ever seen in a commercial theater.

I was mulling this over when the chief appeared, dressed in an elegant blue robe and wearing the traditional Fulani headdress. He stopped just in front of me and stared intently at the screen. He made a strong statement to his aide.

Viewers in Africa are captivated by the "JESUS" film. For many, it is the first film they have ever seen.

"What did he say?" I whispered to our interpreter who was sitting nearby.

"He said, 'That's a white face on the screen, but it's a real Fulani speaking.'"

He was right, of course. We had dubbed the film only a few miles away from that area. And the accent was perfect. Many at the showing did not understand the technology, and we heard questions like, "How do those white men speak Fulani so well?" Any white people they ever heard who spoke their language had an accent. This Jesus spoke their language perfectly.

But then, as He is God's Son, He would be able to speak it perfectly.

When the film ended, one of the young workers picked up a microphone and stepped in front of the screen. He said something like this: "If tonight you would like to become a follower of Jesus, and you would like to ask Him to forgive your sins so that you can live forever with the Creator God, come to the lights."

The string of lights near the screen was turned on. Counselors, who had been trained to explain again the message of Christ, stood under each light, ready to talk with those who came to the front.

Some of the counselors were illiterate. They had been taught what to say by means of a picture book and an audiotape played on a hand-cranked tape recorder. As they turned the crank, the tape explained, "With picture #1, explain that God loves them and offers a wonderful plan for their lives. With picture #2, tell them that man is sinful and thus separated from God. With picture #3, show them that Jesus has come to make the payment for the sins of mankind. And with picture #4, explain that each person must give a personal invitation to Jesus to come into his life, to forgive his sins and become his personal Savior and Lord."

This illiterate village counselor explains the gospel by sharing a picture-book version of the Four Spiritual Laws.

As the film ended, I wondered what would happen. Would anyone come? I had talked with one of the pioneer missionaries to the Fulanis earlier that afternoon and she had been terribly discouraged. Not many of these Muslims had shown much interest. Would it be the same here tonight? I began to pray again.

Then, incredibly, the whole crowd seemed to come toward the lights at once. There were too many people for the counselors to handle. So the film team leader began to counsel them all together using the microphone. Then he led them in a prayer of decision to receive Christ. You could hear the murmuring all across the crowd as one by one they were inviting Jesus on a personal basis to come into their lives.

When the prayer was over, the team leader asked them how many had prayed that prayer with him. It looked like more than 150 lifted their hands in response. We were thrilled. It was only a beginning—but one that was unforgettable.

I would think about it a lot in the days ahead. Wherever people haven't heard the message, someone needs to go. Maybe it should be us.

CHAPTER 9

Dedicated
Film Teams

I n many countries of the world, it is the courageous film
teams who give so many people their only opportunity
to hear of the love and forgiveness of Jesus.

For Daniel Atiyaye in Nigeria and Julio Campos in El Salvador,
the risks have been great. But their love for and commitment to
our Lord have pushed them to keep going.

On a hot, sultry, almost suffocating afternoon, Daniel told me
of his plans for reaching the radical Muslims in the north of
Nigeria. There was no African team leader in whom I had greater
confidence. I asked him about the trips he had made to the north.

"When I worked with one of my first film teams," he said, "I
had a great burden because the Muslims in that area had never
heard the message of Christ. I didn't want anything to interfere
with our efforts to bring them the film. But we had great opposition."

As Daniel and his team drove through their target area for the
showings, young Muslims threw a huge rock at the car, shattering
the windshield. They couldn't see a thing; the car ran off the road,
and they ended up in the middle of a field.

"The glass flew right into our faces. A big shard hit the driver
and sliced almost through his wrist. He needed stitches as soon as
possible. And some of the shattered glass flew into my own eyes."

The police came right away and took the team to the police
station for immediate medical aid. "While we were there, word
came that they had caught those who had thrown the boulder.
They wanted us to stay and testify against the radicals, but I told
them, 'We won't press charges because we have to go and show
the film tonight.'"

The doctor who attended Daniel wanted to remove the glass splinters from his eye immediately. Otherwise, Daniel might go blind.

"No, we can't wait," Daniel protested. "We have been praying to go to this village and many things have tried to stop us. We must go now; we won't wait. I will just pray that God will protect me so we can go and show the film."

The doctor argued with him, but Daniel was adamant and marched out of the police station. The team went to the area they had been praying for and showed the film. Several hundred people received Christ.

"Somehow I was able to get to sleep that night," Daniel recalled, "even with the glass in my eye. The next morning when I woke up, I blinked my eyes and looked in a mirror. I saw two little pieces of glass in the corner of my eye. I brushed them out with my little finger, and my eyes are just fine. God took care of me."

■ ■ ■ ■ ■

Across the world in El Salvador, Julio Campos clutched the guide ropes as the hanging bridge swung crazily in the wind. Only fifty more yards to go, but the weight of the generator in the home-made backpack threatened to throw him off balance. He looked down through the rotten wood bridge slats at the Lempa River far below, and his stomach churned.

"We're not going to stop showing the 'JESUS' film until all of El Salvador has been covered by the gospel," he had told his friends. "No matter what the obstacles are in getting there!" The mountain villages they would visit on this trip were so remote that the people had never seen a film, had never had electricity, and, most importantly, had never heard that Jesus alone forgives sin.

Julio forced himself forward, inching one cautious step at a time. At the far end of the bridge waited Adolfo, his partner in the "JESUS" Film Mountain Brigade, and a local pastor. Julio finally reached him.

They loaded the film equipment on two burros and began climbing the steep mountain path. Several hours later the caravan entered a small valley. A handful of tile-roofed houses dotted the coffee fields.

El Salvador "brigades" take the film by burro into the mountain villages.

That night, four hundred people held their breath as the generator cranked up, and crickets chirped in the distance. Light flashed on the screen, music played, and for the first time ever, Jesus began speaking to the farmers of the village of Buenos Aires.

An El Salvadoran soldier pauses to watch the "JESUS" film.

Julio thought back to the moment on the bridge. It had been scary, but this showing was worth it. He decided anew: No way would he stop until every last centimeter of El Salvador had been covered by the gospel!

Reaching "every last centimeter" of the El Salvador territory hadn't been easy.

Since 1979 a civil war had torn the country apart, and hundreds of thousands of people had been killed.

But in the midst of the chaos, Adonai Leiva, Campus Crusade director in El Salvador, had developed a strategy that fit the war-torn area: He instituted the "JESUS" Film Mountain Brigades. He challenged valiant young men from local churches, most in their teens, to join a mountain brigade and travel from village to village showing the film. These "soldiers of the Lord" committed themselves to proclaim the gospel—no matter how difficult, no matter how dangerous.

"The hard times and sacrifices don't bother us," said Aníbal, a brigade member in the dangerous province of Chalatenango. "We don't eat or sleep well. There are a lot of mosquitos. But it doesn't matter because of the task we have in front of us."

These film team workers in Latin America who are under the direction of Rolando Justiniano are unusually committed. In every new village, they have to meet with town officials for permission to show the film. Then they get local churches involved, if they exist. They also do personal evangelism and train counselors to do the same and to follow up. In many places, heavy religious prejudice precedes them, creating situations of real danger. In other places, national unrest and war threaten their lives.

Under the most unpredictable and sometimes frightening circumstances, these workers show the film, guide nonbelievers to new relationships with Christ, and begin discipleship groups that continue long after the team has moved on to the next village.

Almost all film teams are composed of national workers from their own countries who speak the language. During the summer, these nationals are augmented with short-term workers who come in from North America and other areas of the world.

The film teams in El Salvador have brought peace and reconciliation in the name of Jesus. After six years of sending mountain brigades to every "centimeter," nearly half the population of the country, some two million people, heard this message via the "JESUS" film. About 100,000 have indicated decisions to follow Christ. The "JESUS" film has sparked a great awakening, so much so that 30 percent of the people who have become Christians have joined local churches.

The moral and ethical fabric of the country has begun to change. The general population has begun to feel that it is wrong to torture and kill people. According to a government study, the evangelical presence directly created the conditions that made peace possible because people were willing to forgive and trust each other.

I am continually amazed at the creativity of the teams and those who give direction to the distribution and showing of the film, whether by 16mm film or video. The strategies developed in various parts of the world are ingenious and extremely productive.

In East Africa, national film teams are organizing showings in the schools of Malawi. With 25 percent of the population now testing positive for the AIDS virus, government leaders believe that the only solution is to teach the children of the country to live a sexually pure life. The staff combine the message of abstinence found in Josh McDowell's materials on "Why Wait?" with a curriculum on morals and ethics and the showing of the "JESUS" film.

In Latin America, a massive project is underway to provide "JESUS" videos and films to the exploding church in Cuba. Authorities have not permitted showings outside church properties, so the courageous Christians have erected the screens on the rooftops of their churches, and thousands of people in the street "accidentally" view the film.

In Europe, the staff have conducted campaigns to give the "JESUS" video to every household in Switzerland and Holland. In media-sophisticated countries, this is an unusually effective approach. Plans for additional city-wide and country-wide campaigns are already under way.

In South Africa, leaders prayed for an opportunity to present the film at the annual Easter gathering of one of the country's largest indigenous churches. They suspected that many who were involved in the church were sincere in their search for God, but had little assurance of their eternal salvation.

Finally, arrangements were made. On two successive nights, a million people poured into a valley to view the "JESUS" film in Zulu and Tswana, a half million each night. It was a logistical masterpiece. Seven drive-in-size screens were erected across the

*This crowd in East Africa of more than 30,000 people
exploded in applause at the resurrection of Jesus.*

bottom of a valley. From the hillsides, the picture was visible for
more than half a mile.

Three projectors were used for each screen to ensure that the
film would go on even if one of them broke. The seven locations
were connected by supervisors with walkie-talkies, so that they
would all start the film simultaneously.

The sound came from only one of the projectors and was
piped through 160 powerful speakers placed every hundred me-
ters across the valley. No matter where people went, they could
hear the words of Jesus echoing across the mountainsides.

Very few showings are this spectacular. Most of them range in
size from five hundred to a thousand people. In restricted countries, they are much smaller and may be limited to just a few
people watching very guardedly in their homes. But the response
to the gospel is just as dramatic.

The volume of people now showing the film is doubling and
tripling each year. Besides our own sponsored teams, more than
1,500 organizations are showing it. They are formulating their
own plans, strategies, and dreams. We believe this film belongs to
the whole body of Christ, and we want to help every Christian

ministry reach the people and language groups for whom they have a burden.

Each month, reports of praise come from scores of missions —the Southern Baptist International Mission Board, Christian and Missionary Alliance, OMS International, Mission Aviation Fellowship, United World Mission, Operation Mobilization, CB International, Evangelical Free Church, Every Home for Christ, SIM International, Church of the Nazarene, Pentecostal Assemblies of Canada, Samaritan's Purse, Youth With a Mission, and many, many more.

Everywhere the film has gone, dramatic expansion has taken place. Catholic parishes in Poland have shown it to more than seven million people. The last worldwide priests' retreat at the Vatican offered the film as a "very powerful tool for evangelization." Father Tom Forrest heads a movement of evangelization dedicated to bringing people back to Jesus.

The Holy Ghost Fathers have taken the film to the remote corners of Tanzania. In Togo, the Assemblies of God has planted scores of new churches through the film showings. Twenty-three new Baptist churches were planted through showing the film in Bangladesh.

In Calcutta, India, in Mother Teresa's Homes for the Dying, the film is shown in three different languages. For many who are near death, it is the last opportunity they have to place their faith in the Lord Jesus.

In a high-security prison in South America, Prison Fellowship took the film into a cell block of men who were known as the most vicious killers in that country. Several of them had murdered their own mothers. Prison officials would not go into the dungeon area with them. The Fellowship workers would have to be locked in the cell block with their equipment—if they wanted to take the chance.

At the end of the showing, more than half the men indicated that they wanted to receive the forgiveness of Jesus for their terrible sins.

Every one of the film teams are tremendously dependent on the projectors and the showing equipment. As we launched the film showings in some of the more remote areas of the world, we quickly saw the need to develop equipment that would withstand even the toughest conditions.

At our central equipment warehouse in Orlando, Florida, Mark Steinbach and Dan Noland oversee a team of technicians who build and assemble the equipment packages. Sixteen millimeter projectors are shipped in by the hundreds from Japan.

Each projector is systematically taken apart and a new 100-watt amplifier is built into the same casing to power a sound system that can handle large crowds. Then electrical surge protectors and voltage regulators are added to guard the equipment against burning out from the power surges and voltage spikes that are found in many developing countries. Finally, many of the connections are re-soldered to make sure they continue to work even after hours of bouncing over rocky terrain.

Then the elements of the equipment package are gathered together: sailcloth screens, screen frames made of PVC pipe, projector stands, extra speakers, microphone, power cords, a generator, light cords, extra bulbs, nylon rope to anchor the screen frame, shipping cases, and much more. Finally, there is the extremely tough and challenging job of getting it shipped and cleared through customs in some of the most hostile countries on earth.

I think we have a limited view of what a missionary really is. One of the greatest needs in the evangelization of the world in the coming decade will be for men and women to whom God has given special technical skills—such as engineering, programming, or administration. The film teams around the world need these invaluable, skilled people working in support positions to back them up.

The mission becomes clearer with each passing month. We must recruit teams of workers, donors, technicians, translators, managers—and people who will pray. And we need to keep moving to places where people have not yet heard the gospel.

Sometimes these areas are extremely hostile toward the Good News.

CHAPTER 10

Not an Easy Task

Until recently, it has been very difficult to show the "JESUS" film openly in the country of Nepal. In 1976 there were only five hundred known believers in the entire country, and to change from the religion of one's father was punishable by at least one year in jail. To be caught sharing one's faith was punishable by six years in prison. Occasionally, as many as forty and fifty believers at a time were in jail. Not long ago, money was sent to bail out Christians who had been imprisoned for sharing the *Four Spiritual Laws.*

I have not met any more courageous believers anywhere in the world than in Nepal. One of these, we'll call Joshua, is the leader of all the film teams in that country.

He came from a Brahmin family. As a high school student, he wondered about his purpose in life. Everything seemed hopeless, without meaning. One night someone invited him to a Christian meeting and the speaker's subject was "What Is the Meaning of Life?"

"I don't remember much of what he said that night," Joshua told me, "but I began my search in earnest, and I began to be seriously interested in Jesus." Not long afterward, he committed his life to Christ. Two years later, over the staunch objections of his Hindu parents, he became a staff member of Campus Crusade for Christ.

When I met him, he had already shown the "JESUS" film more than a thousand times in the Hindi language—a thousand showings of an evangelistic film in a country where open evangelism is punishable by five years in prison. A thousand times when a disgruntled Hindu or government informer could have turned him in at any point.

"Isn't it dangerous?" I asked.

103

He smiled. "We must be careful."

The understatement of the year, I thought.

One night he was asked by a gang leader if he would show the film at the leader's birthday party. "I was worried," Joshua said, "because the house was only a few hundred yards from the police station. But the gang leader said, 'We control this area. I'll take care of the police.'"

As they set up the projector, the crowd began to overflow the house, and the gang leader instructed, "Let's move it out into the street."

Outside, Joshua saw two policemen who had passed out. Apparently, the gang leader had drugged them. He told Joshua, "They'll be so embarrassed when they wake up in the morning that they won't say anything against us."

That night, they blocked off both ends of the road, and more than three thousand people came to the showing. The next day, in the tea houses, people were saying, "You see how powerful these Christians are getting? There are so many of them now, and they are showing these films about Jesus."

Well, there probably weren't a lot of Christians there that night, but because the "JESUS" film was being shown openly, it became more acceptable for the local people to consider the claims of Christ. And when the film is shown that openly, people begin to think, *Maybe we're not as much against Christianity as we used to be.*

■ ■ ■ ■ ■

On a crisp Sunday morning in the spring, I made my way to the warehouse where believers were meeting in secret. The snowy peaks of the Himalayas glistened in the sunlight. We were in the outskirts of Kathmandu, on the "roof of the world." During the waning hours of Saturday afternoon, I had walked the narrow, winding streets of the city. I was sure they had remained unchanged through the centuries. Camel caravans, mountain-climbing trekkers, and drug-numbed Western wanderers milled through the labyrinth of streets that made up the old section of the city.

Many had come searching—perhaps for fulfillment in the thrill of climbing Everest or one of the other Himalayan peaks, perhaps for some solace in drugs or in the chants of a Buddhist priest or religious guru.

For me, it was a chance to be with some of the most courageous brothers and sisters in the world. We had just finished the Nepali version of "JESUS" and we would premiere it during my time in Nepal. I was thrilled to be with "Daniel," the director of our ministry for the whole country. His commitment had already cost him two months in prison.

These prisons were terrible hell-holes, with dirt floors and a bucket at the end of the cell for sanitation. As the government troops heard of people being baptized, they picked them up in groups and threw them into prison. The Christian brothers and sisters brought food and blankets to help them survive their year there. They counted it a privilege to suffer for their Lord.

Daniel himself was facing five years of imprisonment. He had already been convicted in court, but the sentencing had not yet been carried out. It was only a matter of time. But he wouldn't be stopped. He continued to plan how all of Nepal could be reached with the message of Jesus.

In his bag, he carried a small, hand-drawn map showing the locations of more than four hundred house churches that he had helped start. He was trying to mobilize all the Christians in Nepal for the cause.

"We ask all Christians to tithe their time," he smiled. "That means we ask them to give thirty-six days a year to go to other areas to share Christ and to show the 'JESUS' film."

His round, smiling face was alive with enthusiasm, courage, and the love of God. *We are missing so much in our own country, in our self-serving American society,* I mused. *We, too, ought to tithe our lives. If we think we are going to live for seventy years, we ought to give the Lord the first seven right off the top, as soon as we are grown-up enough to do it.*

"I just talked with two workers who were in the mountains," Daniel said, interrupting my thoughts. "They found a group of people up there who said they had decided to become followers of Jesus, and they wanted to be baptized. I had asked the men to go and check them out, and if they were sincerely trusting the death and resurrection of Jesus for their salvation, to baptize them. I also asked them to let me know how many they baptized."

These two were not educated men and really didn't know how to keep track of large numbers, so they decided to put a rock on the shore for each person they baptized. That afternoon, these men had returned from a two-day bus ride down the mountain with two huge sacks of stones representing more than two hundred and fifty people they had baptized in the mountain stream.

The church was just getting started in Nepal. Although things have changed in the last few years, at that time there were no denominations. It was just the church at Kathmandu, the church at Patan, or the church at Pokhara.

Their worship practices were taken from all over the world. They prayed like the Koreans, all of them standing and praying out loud at the same time. And, like the Koreans, the men sat on one side of the room and the women on the other. Some of their songs of worship were from the West. And they read extensive portions of Scripture aloud, as I had seen done in other countries. It was an important practice because not many at that time could afford an entire Bible.

Since it was illegal to have a church, the believers had to be very careful. The warehouse we visited was owned by one of the families in the church. Nothing indicated that it was anything other than a warehouse. But when hundreds of people packed into that little area on that Sunday morning, it was transformed into a little bit of heaven on earth.

Being a part of it refreshed me spiritually. The vitality of the young church was inspiring. There were no thousand-year-old traditions here that had to be carried on.

With the rapid growth of the home Bible studies and the beginning of many new churches, some unique and humorous situations arose. One question was: "What should you say at a marriage ceremony of two Nepali believers?"

In some Christian weddings, the bride and groom stood before an elder of the church as he read the *Four Spiritual Laws*. This simple explanation of the gospel shows an illustration of a life with Christ sitting on the throne of one's life and another illustration where ego, or self, is directing the life.

The elder then said something like, "We believe that Christ must be on the throne of each life if the marriage is to be successful. If each person's ego runs his life, the marriage will fail."

Next, the elder turned to the bride and then to the groom and asked, "Is Jesus on the throne of your life?" If they both said yes, he pronounced them married.

So far, in the church of Nepal there have been no divorces!

■■■■■

In other parts of the world, the continual political uprisings, coups, and factional wars put the team members in constant danger. During the fighting in Liberia, one of the teams attempted to escape across the border in the company of a large group of refugees. They had stopped for the night when rebel soldiers suddenly attacked. With little thought or reason, the rebels began killing people at will.

The rebels ordered the film team leader to lie down in the dirt, and one rebel put a rifle to the side of the team leader's head. They demanded the keys to the film van. Surprisingly, when he gave them the keys, they let him go. After several days of walking, the team crossed the border into Sierra Leone and temporary safety.

In Zaire, the armed soldiers of the rebels simply stopped the "JESUS" film truck and took it. Fortunately, no one was shot and the team had not yet picked up the projectors and equipment.

In the Muslim Middle East, it becomes difficult to recount the hardships faced by the workers. As I write today, I know my words could actually endanger the lives of certain workers if I were to list specific locations or countries.

The director of the "JESUS" film teams all across North Africa and the Middle East is one of the most courageous of these workers. Most of the nearly one billion Muslims of the world live in the countries for which he is responsible. Two of these are Iraq and Iran.

As I met with the workers in that area of the world, I was impressed with their great faith in the middle of the most repressive and dangerous circumstances I could envision. Every religion of the world teaches tolerance—except Islam. Within Islam, there are those who teach that Allah will be pleased if you kill Christians who try to spread the message of Jesus.

In one of the Muslim countries of the former Soviet Union, one of our workers attended a meeting with the Minister of Religious Affairs. When a missionary appealed to him to enforce the constitutional provision of freedom of religion, he simply sneered, "If you do not leave our country, I will kill you. That's what I think of your freedom of religion."

Yet, the workers keep going. They report that they meet people everywhere who tell them that Jesus has appeared to them in a dream and simply said, "I am the way to God." In Algeria, six young men in the same village had the same dream. Through a series of circumstances, they found out about each other and are now meeting regularly in a group to learn more about this person called Jesus.

I talked with one of our workers in Iran who said, "Ayatollah Khomeini was the best thing that ever happened to Iran. He demonstrated the viciousness and hopelessness of Islam, and it is driving people to Jesus."

He told me that his phone was tapped and someone was listening to every call. In the war between Iran and Iraq, many Iranians had returned with legs blown off because of the mines that Saddam Hussein had spread everywhere. When these men returned to Tehran, the government assigned a number of them to be phone monitors and listen to the calls of suspected Christians.

One day our worker received a call from a person saying he was disillusioned with Islam and needed to learn more about Jesus. He said he wanted to know how he could be forgiven for his sins so that God would accept him when he died.

Suddenly the man monitoring the call forgot he was supposed to be silent, and he blurted out, "Yes, I'd like to know about that, too." Within minutes, he heard a clear presentation of the gospel.

A week after the Gulf War ended, I received a fax from Baghdad asking us to send two thousand "JESUS" videos in the Arabic language. I replied that I was sure they would be confiscated in customs, and that we could not send them without a clearance given by the government. Seven days later, we received the letter of clearance from the government giving us permission to import videos on the life of Jesus. Why? I have no idea, except that God is at work. He is not willing that any should perish. His will is that every person in the world hear the message of His love and forgiveness through Jesus Christ before He returns.

Therefore, I believe in the decade ahead we will see the opening of China and the penetration of the entire Muslim world with the gospel. Things may tighten again after that, but it could be that in our generation we will see the literal fulfillment of Matthew 24:14, where Jesus said that the gospel of the kingdom will be preached for a witness to all the nations, then the end will come. There is no wall or curtain or regime that is too difficult for the power of God to pierce.

A few months after the war, a pastor from the United States got an appointment with Saddam Hussein. At the end of their meeting, Saddam asked him, "What do you want me to do for you?"

"I want you to permit the 'JESUS' film to be shown on national television," he replied.

Hussein agreed. And on Christmas day the "JESUS" film was broadcast nationwide to the eighteen million people of Iraq. How could this happen? In human terms, it is unexplainable. God did it!

He is at work, and the gates of hell will not prevail against Him and His children. Since it is God's will that the whole world hear of Jesus, we know that they will! It is the surest thing in the universe. The fact that He might use the "JESUS" film as one method to bring His message to those who have never heard is simply a tribute to His grace. It encourages us to be faithful stewards of the film and to make sure that the glory for all that is accomplished goes to God.

A group of people called the Kurds inhabit northern Iraq. They began fighting against Saddam Hussein for their survival almost as soon as "Desert Storm" was over. They want to form their own country called Kurdistan. Saddam would like to wipe them out or drive them into Turkey.

In the middle of this chaos, we began to dub the "JESUS" film into five of the Kurdish languages. As one of the voice actors was reading the script, he spoke of a legend that says one of his ancestors was one of the kings of the East, from among the Medes, who went to worship the baby Jesus. This man had never seen a Bible, but with perfect accuracy he told the story, handed down from generation to generation, of the Magi who came to worship Jesus in the first century.

The Kurds are descendants of the ancient Medes who apparently once worshipped Jesus. My prayer is that the Kurds will return to their heritage and thus become one of the first Muslim people groups to return en masse to their roots and follow Christ.

CHAPTER 11

It's All About People

Being born spiritually into the family of God and becoming a follower of Jesus is the most unique, personal, and fulfilling relationship a person can ever have. Many people see the film repeatedly, but for each one it is again an individual time of reflection. The person is given another opportunity to consider his response to the message of love and forgiveness that he is hearing.

People don't always respond to Christ the first time they see the film. But because 70 percent of the film is simply Luke's Gospel, taken from the Word of God, it does not return void. Sometimes it takes time for people to really understand what Jesus is saying, or to realize they have a need that only Jesus can fill.

One night we showed the film to nearly five hundred people in the mountains outside Tijuana, Mexico. When it ended, the leader of the film team announced, "If tonight you would like to become a follower of Jesus, and receive Him as your personal Savior and Lord, come to the light!"

I took out my Spanish *Four Spiritual Laws* booklet that explained, very simply, how a person could begin a relationship with Christ, and I went to the lights where the men were gathered. I began to talk to a young man there who was in his twenties. "What did you think of the film?"

"I liked it very much. I saw it before."

I was curious. "Oh, really? Where did you see it?"

"About seven hundred miles south of here near Tampico, five or six months ago."

"Did you invite Christ to come into your life then when you saw it?"

"No, I didn't. But tonight I want to."

So I opened the *Four Spiritual Laws* booklet and began to read it with him. We walked through each law, step by step. At the end, he said he would like to pray the prayer of invitation and receive Christ.

After we finished the prayer, I talked with him a little more about his background. "Why didn't you receive Christ the first time you saw the film?"

He shrugged. "I don't know. I was rebellious, I guess, against God." He told me what happened after he left there. "I got involved with drugs. Not too long after I saw the film, I was shot by cocaine runners who were delivering drugs from Colombia to the United States." He opened his shirt and showed me the scars from four bullet holes in his chest.

"There is no possible way I should be here today," he sighed. "As I lay in the dust with the blood pouring out of my body, I cried out to God to save me, and He did. I'm here only because of God, and I want to give my life back to Him right now."

I turned to another page in the back of the booklet and said, "Let me show you what it says about you in the Scripture. John 1:12 says that when you receive Him, you become a child of God, His son. Did you receive Him tonight?"

"Yes," he nodded.

"Well, what does that make you, according to what this verse in the Bible says?"

"His son," he replied with some amazement.

"That's right," I confirmed. "And when I made this same commitment a number of years ago, what did I become?"

"You became a son of God as well."

"Then what's our relationship with each other?" I asked.

"Somos hermanos," he beamed. "We're brothers."

I shook his hand, and said, "Welcome to the family! Let me introduce you to some of our other brothers and sisters." I took him to some of the other counselors who were with us, and introduced him. About thirty minutes later, after talking to those who were with us, he turned to leave. As he faded into the darkness, he waved slightly and smiled, "Adios, familia!"

He understood what it means to be in the family of God!

■ ■ ■ ■ ■

But coming into the family is not always easy.

One night in a little village in Ghana, gangsters broke into young Miriam's house. Her father and brother tried to protect the family, but they could not stop the savage attack. The gunmen killed her father instantly with a bullet to the head, and they tied up her brother. For the next three hours they beat and raped Miriam and her mother. Her brother began to lose his mind as the crazed attackers forced him to watch the brutal rapes.

Finally, the gunmen left. Miriam's brother walked around with a vacant stare, unable to function. Her mother became desperately sick. Where could Miriam possibly turn for help?

At this point, some businessmen came into the town and offered Miriam a job in the city of Abidjan, the capital of Ivory Coast. It was a nearby country and she needed the work, so she took the job.

When she arrived in Abidjan, she discovered that she had been hired to work in a brothel. But now she owed the men money for the transportation, and they would not let her leave. She immediately began to plot her escape. It would not be easy—she was watched continually. Finally, three days later, an opening came and in panic and desperation Miriam raced out of the brothel and into the dark, back streets of the city.

"As I was running down a dark alley," she told us later, "I heard some music. I ran into the building where the music was playing, and I found out it was coming from the film 'JESUS.' I stayed and watched the whole film.

"At the end of it, I accepted Jesus as my personal Savior. One of the counselors said he would help me get a good job, and I'm now working in one of the hotels here in the city."

And so, in the midst of a world where people are sometimes extremely cruel, abusive, and exploitive, one more young woman has found a new hope in life—and has felt the touch of Jesus.

For a couple in India, the discovery of Jesus came amid deep pain.

One day I stood on the banks of the Ganges River in the north of India. On one side sat the temple of the monkey god and on the other side, a Hindu temple. I was talking with several local Christians about how many people are searching for spiritual life and hope, and how important it is that we keep showing the film until every last person has been reached.

One of the men, a worker, spoke up as if to underline the urgency of the task. "I came out here to this part of the river just a few weeks ago. Near the river I saw a man and a woman obviously in tremendous distress. The woman was weeping uncontrollably.

"When I asked her what was wrong, she couldn't talk, but her husband said, 'We have been seeking peace for a long time in our lives. The Hindu priest in our village said that the only way we could find peace was to throw our two-year-old baby into the river. So just a little while ago we threw our little son into the river.'"

The worker explained how they could find true, eternal peace and led the couple to place their faith in Jesus Christ. Their last words as they left were, "If only you had come thirty minutes sooner, our little boy would still be alive."

In Sabah, the northern part of Borneo in East Malaysia, the jungles that rise out of the blue Pacific were at one time inhabited by cannibals. As we went in there for the premiere of the film, in the Kadazan Dusun language, we were assured that the cannibals were long since gone. But the day we arrived in the capital city, Kota Kinabalu, the headlines on the paper read, "Headless Corpse Found in Kota Kinabalu."

However, this was not a time for fear. This was the opening of the gospel to another unreached group of people. During the next three days, more than eight thousand people came out for the premiere showings in the Kadazan Dusun language. Of these, three thousand indicated decisions to receive Christ. We had large showings in some of the major cities, and then one night we went into a primitive, rural village.

When we arrived, our host ushered us to his home. We removed our shoes and climbed the creaky steps to a little house built on poles. They had no furniture, no beds—just a few rolled-up mats and a few extra clothes hanging on a rope. The kitchen was nothing more than a lean-to shed with some hanging pots, cooking coals, and a few plates and utensils. Yet these believers were so excited that we had brought the film in their language that they insisted on preparing a banquet for us of sticky rice, fresh vegetables, a little chicken, and a few mystery dishes.

By the time we finished dinner, hundreds of people had walked out of the jungle to the clearing. They were curious to see the film we would screen on a bedsheet hanging from the side of one of the barns. Cattle and caribou, which were used to pull the plows through rice paddies, were feeding nearby.

As the sun sank in the western sky, people began to walk across little dikes through the rice paddies to this hillside barn. They seated themselves in the soft grass, and waited for the film to start.

Rain began to fall. We quickly hustled the projector underneath a covering. The people sat in the rain anyway, and we began showing the film. At the end, we asked those who wanted to respond to come to the lights so they could make their commitment to follow Jesus of Nazareth as their Savior.

One of those who came was an eighty-year-old woman. A counselor who spoke English brought her to me. "This lady would like to meet you, because she knows you are the one who helped to make the film and bring it here tonight."

The old lady turned her face up toward me and said, "Many, many years ago when I was a small girl, a missionary came through our area and talked about Jesus as the way that we could know God. But I never knew how I could accept Jesus. With this film you have told me how to open the door of my life and invite Him to come in. I'm so happy, and I want you to know that tonight I have opened my door."

I looked down at her. She was about 4 feet 10 inches tall, with a wrinkled face and paper-thin skin. But she had a radiance on her face that could come only from having discovered this wonderful news, even though it had happened so late in her life. Now she knew that she would live forever. And she was ecstatic.

This, I thought, is what this ministry is all about. One person who finds out that she can know Jesus, that she can live forever, because of what He did on the cross two thousand years ago. It is worth giving your life for a cause like this. An eighty-year-old woman would live eternally because we had brought Jesus this night to a little village in Borneo.

In Mexico, Ghana, India, and Borneo, people have responded to the gospel when they have seen "JESUS." But for them and millions of others in dozens of countries, this is just the beginning. After each film showing, the follow-up process begins for every new believer. The follow-up strategy of Campus Crusade for Christ establishes training centers to prepare leaders for the newly established convert groups. I saw my first training center in Asia...

CHAPTER 12

Following Up

Northwest Thailand had been Buddhist for generations, virtually untouched by the wonderful words of Jesus. Mile after mile of rice paddies were broken only by small clumps of trees that sheltered the little villages of the farmers. A rooster crowed in the distance as I rolled over in my sleeping bag and looked out across the countryside around Phuket. Dawn was breaking on the far horizon. A new day.

A few feet away, I spied the mosquito net of Boonma Panthasri, the director for the Campus Crusade for Christ ministry in Thailand. He had jerry-rigged a little tent out of the netting, and was on his knees reading the Bible and praying. I knew he had been up for hours, and I felt convicted about my own meager prayer life.

For Thai Christians, prayer is absolutely essential. Evil spirits have held this land captive for generations. "We must break their stranglehold on the hearts of the people through prayer before we go to talk to them," Boonma told me later. "We go to the 'prayer mountain' for three days every month, and we begin each day with an hour of prayer. It is the source of our strength."

I knew he was right. I had seen the "spirit houses" built by each person who had a home. They were little dollhouse-like miniatures set on a pole in the corner of their property. According to tradition, all the land had once belonged to the evil spirits. And they would harass the people and cause sickness and death in their families unless they appeased them. The people did this by building the evil spirits a little house of their own and bringing offerings of food to them regularly. The eaves of the people's own houses were designed with sharp-pointed sticks protruding to spear any spirits who tried to get in under the eaves.

This "spirit house" in Thailand was built by villagers to protect themselves from demons.

This was not the sanitized, don't-offend-anyone Christianity of the West. This was the kind of faith that acknowledged that this really is a spiritual world. Powerful forces of darkness seek to blind people to the wonderful salvation found in the living, forgiving God of the universe.

I had wondered about the reports from Thailand of encounters with demons, and of dramatic healings after prayer. Observing Boonma in this early morning hour, I saw again the source of their power.

The film team workers in the area were not professional pastors or mission leaders. They were rice farmers, school teachers, and young graduates who had found freedom from fear and hope for eternal life through Jesus. Now, as they met people who were bound by demon possession or were on sickbeds, they simply prayed for them. And God was pleased to release the oppressed and heal them. They never talked about it. It wasn't so special. They worshipped the Almighty God by affirming that He could do anything. I marveled at their depth of understanding and their simple faith.

When the film began showing in Thailand, it had been in great demand. In the first five years, the teams showed it to more than four million people. They helped set up small Bible study fellowships, called New Life Groups, to meet in village homes where people could learn how to grow in their new Christian faith.

The need for leaders rapidly outstripped the supply. There simply weren't enough mature Christians to lead all of these new converts. At that time, Boonma began establishing New Life

New Life Groups are formed to help new believers grow in their faith.

Training Centers. They were at the heart of the follow-up and discipleship efforts after every "JESUS" film showing.

When we came to the Phuket New Life Training Center in Thailand in early summer, we saw an old store that had been rented for a month.

Boonma gave me the tour. "The men sleep at night on this floor. In the morning, they roll up their mats and we have our training class in this same room. The women stay upstairs. We have thirty trainees at this time. They will be here for one month. We also have six trainers, so that means we have one trainer for each five trainees."

I wandered outside where some of the trainees were relaxing during a break. Our little visiting group had disrupted their schedule temporarily, but it seemed to be all right with them. They didn't often see people from America in their little village. I talked with some of them through my interpreter. A young woman named Srithadee told me her story.

She was twenty-four years old. There were no Christians in her village. It was controlled by Communist guerrillas. Earlier in the year, her uncle had told her about Jesus for the first time.

This New Life Training Center in Thailand helps prepare leaders for the thousands of New Life Groups being formed through the showing of the "JESUS" film.

Then, on May 24, a worker from the training center had explained the gospel to her through the *Four Spiritual Laws* booklet, and she had prayed to receive Christ.

Eager to know how to talk to others about this new faith she had found, she asked the trainer who had led her to Christ if she could enter the training center that day. The classes had just begun, so they included her.

"What do you do here at the training center?" I asked.

She smiled shyly. "We have our personal prayer time in the morning from 5:00 to 6:00. Then we have our group prayer time and breakfast. Classes go all morning until noon. In the afternoon we do field work where we talk to people about Jesus. At night we show the 'JESUS' film, and we start Bible study groups."

"How many people do you talk to about Christ each day?" I inquired.

"I'm not sure," she said slowly. "I just go from shop to shop and house to house. Probably six or eight people each day."

"Have you been able to bring anyone to Christ?" I wondered if I had made a mistake in asking this question of such a new believer. I didn't want to discourage her.

She brightened immediately. "Oh yes."

"Do you know how many?" I asked as the ever-analyzing, statistical Westerner.

"I'm not sure." She hesitated. "Let's see. There were three housewives, two men in the shops, three policemen, four teenagers, and this morning I led a man to Christ in the jail."

I counted them up: thirteen. I looked again at today's date: June 7. She had been a Christian for only thirteen days. In her first thirteen days as a believer, she had introduced thirteen others to Christ. No wonder the church was exploding in northeast Thailand.

"Is there anything you would like us to pray about for you?" I wondered. I considered asking her to pray for *me*.

Her eyes seemed to dim as she replied. "You can pray for my family. I am the only Christian. And you can pray for my village. I would like to bring my village to Jesus." She paused for my interpreter. "And pray for all of Thailand to know Christ."

"We'll pray," I promised, pretending to fix my contact lens as I wiped a tear from my eye. This was the essence of the first-century church. In a little village that lacked much of the material things of life, the vibrancy, the spiritual freshness, and the unbridled expectancy were absolutely breathtaking. This was Christianity in its purest form—naive, clean, and trusting. These were my kind of people.

The church was born out of adversity and spiritual darkness, but it would last forever. Srithadee was one of its new spiritual children. And she was born running.

As we bounced along a country road some hours later, I asked Boonma to tell me more about the training centers. "Is the training the same everywhere?"

"The training sessions all consist of 150 hours," he explained. "Half of this is spent in the classroom, and half of it in the field. Some of our training centers are like this one where people come for a month and live in." In the cities, the training sessions last about four months. "We meet twice a week in the evenings, and all day on Saturdays until we complete the same content."

"What's the objective of the training?"

"We want the trainees to become spiritual multipliers. We want them to be able to lead others to Christ, know how to follow up on them personally and challenge them to attend a discipleship group, and then be able to teach this group the same things until they have also introduced others to Christ."

"How many people do these trainees talk to each day?" I probed, telling him about my conversation with Srithadee.

"We would like each person to lead three people to Christ every day—twenty-one people each week," he answered.

I wondered if I had heard him correctly.

"You mean, you want them to *talk* to three people each day? You can't control how many people will make decisions to receive Christ."

"No. You are right that we can't control how many people will decide for Christ, but if we talk to enough people, we should see twenty-one come to the Lord each week."

The questions were coming up in my mind faster than I could ask them. "How many do you have to talk with to see twenty-one people make commitments?"

"You should talk to several hundred," he said matter-of-factly.

"But how can one person talk to several hundred in a week?"

"In groups," he explained. "In our countryside, we have big families, and they live very close to one another. So when you go into a home, it is easy to get twenty or thirty family members gathered. Then you can explain to all of them about Jesus and how they can become a part of His family and have their sins forgiven."

Again I realized my narrow view of the world. Whole families were coming to the Lord. New believers were fearless in their witnessing. There weren't any "older" Christians around to tell them that it was difficult to share their faith, or that people weren't interested, or that you should talk with people one at a time, or any of a host of other discouraging things. In the first excitement of their new-found faith, they simply were passing it on, and many were coming into the kingdom.

"How do you do your personal witnessing?" I asked Boonma.

"I remember that it is always best to be interested in other people first. So I go to the house of a rice farmer and I meet him outside his house. I tell him his rice fields look good and we talk about that. Then I say, 'That is a very nice water buffalo you have,'

Hundreds of new churches have resulted from "JESUS" film showings in Thailand.

or something like that, and we talk some more. After a while he invites me into his house for something to drink.

"After we have talked for awhile, I ask him, 'What are your dreams for the future?' And he tells me that someday he hopes to buy a truck or a tractor. 'And then what?' I ask him. He says he supposes he will die. 'And then what?' I say. And he will say he doesn't know what will happen then.

"At that point, I tell him I used to wonder about that, too, but I have found some good answers in the teachings of Jesus. I ask him if he would like to see these same teachings. He usually says yes, so I read the *Four Spiritual Laws* to him."

It was so easy.. It was simply taking the initiative to talk to others, be interested in them, and see if there would be an opportunity to share the gospel or a personal testimony.

"We believe that everyone can be taught to share their faith," Boonma continued. "That is why we put such great emphasis on the New Life Training Centers. We had one man, though, a vegetable vendor, who would not come to the training center because he could not read. But he asked for a supply of the *Four Spiritual Laws* booklets.

"Every day, as he made his rounds in the village, he would stop and talk with people, saying, 'I cannot read. I wonder if you would read this booklet to me.'

"People would read the gospel presentation to him. He would say, 'Ah, yes, I have opened the door of my life to Jesus. Have you? You'd like to, wouldn't you? Perhaps we could pray that prayer together.'

"This last year," Boonma beamed, "that man has led more than three hundred people to Christ, and he himself cannot read."

These training centers were fantastic launching sites for entire movements of evangelism and the planting of new churches. I was to see the same thing in the West African country of Mali.

Mali sounds like it should be an island in the south Pacific. Far from it. On the southern edge of the Sahara Desert, it's a country of nine million people, and home to the most desolate city on earth, Timbuktu.

I was unprepared, at first, for the dust. My good friend and veteran African missionary, Jim Green, and I had driven by truck for eight hours up the main road between the city of Abidjan in the Ivory Coast and Bamako, the capital of Mali. The road had started as a good four-lane highway, but gradually it narrowed to two lanes, and then to a gravel road, and finally just a track through the bush country. I saw a semi-trailer truck lying on its side. It had hit a hole in the road and simply toppled over. No tow trucks or winches in that part of the world! I wondered how they would ever get it upright.

Mali reminds me of the old films about the French Foreign Legion. The buildings are made of stone. The Tuareg nomads roam the desert wastes in robes and turbans, a lifestyle unchanged since the first century. And dust is everywhere.

A car-wash would do well here, I mused, *if anyone had any money.* But the country is desperately poor. It is rated by the United Nations as one of the toughest places on earth to live. The average annual income is less than $200. Only 20 percent of the people are literate. And it is a Muslim country.

But God is at work. A steady stream of stories of people coming to Christ through the "JESUS" film pours out of the New Life Training Centers. Under the amazing leadership of the Reverend Kassoum Keita, and against impossible odds, the claims of Christ are spreading rapidly and the church is growing.

I walked into the training center in Nosombougou. The walls were made of mud bricks and covered with a thin coating of mud. Running horizontally across the room were what looked like twenty or thirty small, mud walls about 18 inches high and 12 inches wide. I realized that these were benches for the trainees. They would have to hold their notebooks, if they had any, on their laps.

"Time for dinner," Jim called in to me. "Looks like they've made a feast in our honor."

The goat stew, boiled in a pot made from the bottom of an old gas can, was hot and filling, and soon we were off to an evening showing of the film. This one was in the Bambara language.

Kassoum Keita extends the ministry of the film teams in twenty countries of French-speaking Africa.

There were very few vehicles in this area of Mali. We rode on a cart made with an old car axle and pulled by a donkey. But there, under the stars, I again saw the power of God to change people's lives. Most of these Muslims either had never heard of Jesus or else knew virtually nothing about Him.

Now they were making decisions to turn their lives and their entire future over to Him.

As we returned from the showing that night, God gave me a glimpse of what He was doing in this incredible country.

Some time earlier, when many had been on the verge of starvation, Campus Crusade had teamed up with World Vision to help supply food and grain. Instead of setting up the customary feeding center, the workers dispensed grain from the homes of Christians who had learned at the nearby training centers how to share their faith.

During the days, the grain would be dispensed from the homes and the Christians would share their witness. And each evening the "JESUS" film would be shown in a different part of the affected area.

In the first six months of the campaign, more than a thousand Muslims came to Christ.

The Malian film teams and their partners in the New Life Training Centers are committed to starting new churches. In just one year, the teams showed the film 1,486 times to 1.2 million people, with 116,000 indicating decisions for Christ.

More remarkable was the follow-up. New Life discipleship groups numbered 3,934, and 503 new churches were planted. It has always been God's plan that people be brought to maturity in Christ in a local body of believers. There they can be taught "to observe all things I have commanded you," as Jesus said, and the Great Commission in all its dimensions is fulfilled.

But what draws a person to Jesus? For some it is a deep physical need.

CHAPTER 13

The Healing Touch of Jesus

In the village of Rara, Ghana, a crowd of more than three thousand people gathered in anticipation of the film showing. They had never seen a film in their own language of Twi. The children were packed together in front of the screen by the hundreds. Eight- and ten-year-olds held younger brothers and sisters in their laps.

The sticky, oppressive heat of the day began to lift as darkness fell on the village. But the thoughts of the children were not on the heat. They covered the dusty field like a human blanket, a jumble of tiny limbs and once shiny bodies now dulled by suffocating layers of dust and dirt.

In a place where daily survival is the only issue, opportunities to see anything like a feature film in color seldom occur. With parents working continually, children are left to fend for themselves. No bedtime stories. Few hugs and kisses. No tucking into a nice, clean featherbed.

In many of these villages, the children are ignored. A man may marry three or four wives—they can farm for him and people will think he is wealthy. The wives produce children who can work, but the father feels little responsibility for them. So they play in the dirt with sticks and stones and old tin cans.

But not tonight.

On this night, there would be a film in their own language. And they were ready.

As the second reel of the film started, a sudden shout burst from the children, and they scattered as if a bomb had been dropped in their midst. The film team worker looked down to see a giant scorpion with its pinchers open and its deadly tail lifted to sting. The worker pounced on the scorpion and killed it in seconds.

As the film showing continued, the workers gave thanks that no children had been stung. The superstitious villagers would have immediately rejected the film, believing that this strange God had displeased the spirits and that the spirits had sent the scorpion to punish them.

Just a few minutes later, a woman in the crowd began to shout. She was holding a completely rigid baby girl in her arms. She looked down in agony at her ten-month-old infant, wailing, "My baby is dying! My baby is dying!"

The film team leader stopped the film. He and his partner, along with a local pastor and several counselors, took the child, laid hands on her and prayed. "Oh God, You have healed the hump-backed lady," they shouted aloud. "You have healed the blind man. You have raised the daughter of Jairus from the dead. You can heal this baby. Show Your mighty power. Heal this little baby to show Your love, and for Your glory."

The crowd listened and stared in stony silence.

Suddenly the rigid body of the baby went limp in their arms, and she began to cry. They gave her back to her mother and she hugged her to her breast with deep relief.

Then the film team leader turned to the crowd. "What Jesus did on the film, He has done for this little baby girl. Jesus is the most powerful, most loving God in the universe. He can heal you; He can forgive your sins, and He can make it possible for You to live forever with Him. If you want to receive Him as Your personal Savior and Lord, if you want to be healed spiritually, come forward now to the light."

The whole crowd of three thousand began to move at once. It was impossible for them to get any closer. So the film workers counseled them all at one time over the microphone. They prayed a prayer of salvation together.

In a little village in Ghana, Africa, there is a wonderful new hope. They have a new heart, a new Savior, and a new Lord— Jesus!

In hundreds of remote villages each night, this two-hour film on the life of Jesus results in His healing touch on the bodies and hearts of thousands. Eager villagers watch Jesus heal the blind man, the demon-possessed boy, and the hump-backed woman. With childlike faith, some often cry out to Jesus to heal them—and He does!

In a village in Thailand, Sukaret had lain in a hammock for thirteen months, unable to walk. Her friend came to tell her of the film she had seen about the one true God, Jesus. Sukaret said, "If Jesus will heal me, I'll believe in Him."

Her friend, a new believer, bowed her head to the ground and said quietly, "Jesus, please heal my friend so that she can believe in You."

Sukaret got up and walked.

When I met her a few days later, she was attending her first follow-up session for new believers. Twenty new believers sat on straw mats outside a little hut in this village. Sukaret took me over to see the hammock where she had lain for the last year. "I was crippled," she beamed, "but Jesus healed me and now I can walk."

I asked Sawat, the film team leader in Thailand if this was unusual.

"No," he smiled. "Many people are healed by Jesus. Our team was showing the film one night in the Maekaw district in the yard of a school. We put up a loudspeaker so that all the people in the village could hear the movie.

"A sick man lay in a house about four hundred feet from the showing. He heard through the film that Jesus can heal the sick and raise the dead. When he heard this through the loudspeaker, he said to himself, 'Maybe if Jesus is so powerful, I can pray for myself, and I can ask Him to heal me.' His leg was crippled and he could not walk, but he pushed himself up to his knees with his hands and said, 'Jesus, if You are the living and true God and have power to heal sickness, I pray that You heal me now.'

"He was healed right away. He ran to the film showing and found the leader. He told the leader what had happened to him. 'I could not come to the first part of the film, because I could not walk. But now Jesus has healed me, and I am coming to bring you five dollars.'

"The film team leader refused the money, but the man insisted that the team stay at his house overnight. In the morning, he brought all of his family members together so that they could become Christians."

It reminded me of the first-century disciples.

Mrs. Peni of Purwonegoro, Indonesia, had been blind for four years. But someone told her about the "JESUS" film, where Jesus heals a blind man. She asked her youngest daughter to guide her to the film showing so she could hear the story even if she couldn't see the picture.

When the scene was shown where the blind man asks Jesus to heal him, Mrs. Peni shouted out, "I want to see, too!" A few moments later, as the film showed Jesus being nailed to the cross, her vision was restored.

At a town meeting some time later, the Muslim officials wanted to ridicule her and prove that she really had not been healed. They asked her to come to the front and light a candle. Mrs. Peni got up from her seat and confidently strode to the front. Then, as everyone watched, she picked up the matches and lit the candle. Forty more Muslims decided to trust in Christ after seeing her witness.

The film was brought back to the village because everyone wanted to see the film about the man who healed Mrs. Peni. And 3,500 people came to see "JESUS."

She and thirteen others were baptized, half of whom had received Christ as a result of the witness of Mrs. Peni. A new church has now been started in her village.

But it is not the movie that heals. It is the powerful words of Jesus simply brought to the motion picture screen. Jesus is still doing miracles, still changing lives. And this visible work of the Holy Spirit brings awakening to the areas of the world long held in bondage to Buddhism and Islam.

I sat on a straw mat talking with a young man in Thailand. "Why have you decided to be a follower of Jesus, when everyone in your village is a Buddhist?" I asked.

"Let me tell you what Jesus did for me," he answered through my interpreter. "I was hit by a truck, and my leg was broken in three places. I was not able to have it treated properly and gangrene set in. Within a week it had swelled to three times the normal size, and the doctors said I must have it cut off. Even then, they said, I would probably die.

"Then someone came to our village with the 'JESUS' film. I saw Jesus bring the man who was dead back to life. I asked Jesus to heal me, and He did! Now I will follow Him until I do die, even if nobody else in my village believes."

It is wonderful when God heals someone physically. But the changes He makes in the lives of individuals, families, and whole villages is sometimes beyond belief.

A man by the name of Tant lived in the Kalasin province of northeast Thailand. One day his son left home and ran away to Bangkok. Despondent over the loss of his son, Tant often told people, "If I cannot see my son, I would rather die."

He spent his days drinking and his nights with prostitutes.

Some time later, Tant received word that his son had been killed in a bicycle accident. He went crazy and began wandering in the jungle all day crying out, "I want my son. I want my son." He rarely ate, his grief was so great.

One night he had a dream in which an old man appeared to him and said, "If you want your son back, go to the Christian church in the city. They will tell you what to do."

The next morning he went to the city and began searching for a Christian church. On the way he met a Christian. The Christian told him, "Sir, you can meet your son, but you must accept Jesus Christ as your Savior."

The man said, "Who is this Jesus Christ?"

"He is the living and true God and He can give you peace and He can give you eternal life."

Tant bowed his head and received Jesus as his personal Savior. He went back home filled with peace and joy, confident that one day he would see his son again. A short time later, he received a letter in which someone told him that his son had become a Christian in Bangkok just before he died.

Tant began to tell people that he would one day see his son again in heaven. Through his witness, seven families came to the Lord and formed a New Life Group. Tant became the leader. His drinking, smoking, and immorality gone, he was a changed man.

One of his sisters was a Buddhist nun. She heard about the change in his life and came to see, bringing a number of other nuns from the temple with her. She became a Christian, along with three of the nuns. Tant had found a spiritual healing for his heart that gave him a joy he could not contain.

I can't explain the miraculous intervention of God in some lives. I don't know why He sometimes seems to manifest His power and presence in such dramatic ways. I only know that in some cases there is no human explanation for the miracles that accompany the showing of "JESUS." It is the supernatural work of a loving and powerful God.

It was certainly true of a rural village in India.

CHAPTER 14

Simply Supernatural

A young couple from southern India decided that God was calling them to the Pioria region in the north. They took their three-year-old son and went out from the Friends' Missionary Prayer Band to take the gospel to an unreached people called the Maltos. This part of the Bihar state had been known as the "graveyard of missionaries."

For several years, they worked there with no visible results. Everything they tried was opposed. The leaders in the area told people that if any of them believed in Jesus, they would not receive their monthly subsidy from the Indian government.

In addition to the lack of response to everything they did, they experienced a discouraging and debilitating time of illness. The water was infected with disease, and very often the entire family was sick.

One day the father felt especially ill. He went to the doctor to get something to ease his pain. When he came home from the doctor that night, he collapsed on the doorway of his home and died.

The distraught mother tried to figure out what to do. She went in to check on their little boy in bed and found him dead as well. She returned to her home in south India, and it seemed there had been no results from the giving of these lives for the kingdom.

Several weeks later, a "JESUS" film team came into this area and the government officials, instead of stopping it, said, "We want to see this." They had usually stopped anything having to do with Christianity, but the governor of the area, quite impressed with the film, gave his permission for it to be shown, and he said it should be protected.

The film team came to the village where the couple from the Friends' Missionary Prayer Band had lived. The people there said that on the night the missionary died, some clouds had appeared in the sky, and on the clouds a larger-than-life man walked over their barren hills, shedding tears. He went to a tree and picked a branch from it and the branch withered. Finally the picture of the man faded from the sky. The villagers thought perhaps God was displeased with them because they had not accepted the message of the missionary.

When the film team set up the projector, screen, and generator for the showing, the projector wouldn't start. They prayed, claiming Jesus' power over the evil spirits in the area. The equipment began to work again.

When the film reached the point where Jesus is baptized and His face is seen for the first time, the crowd suddenly roared. The team stopped the film to ask what the shouting was about.

"It's him!" they exclaimed. "The man we saw walking in the clouds!"

Most of the villagers came to Christ that night. The people connected the film with the missionary and the man they had seen in the clouds.

The word of Christ began to spread. These new Maltos Christians began reaching their neighboring villages. Within weeks, reports came in of 130 new believers meeting in seven different churches. But this was only the beginning. The power of the evil spirits that had long enslaved the Maltos with fear had been broken. They began to see people healed and demons cast out. In the first eighteen months after that miraculous event, more than 6,500 Maltos believers were baptized.

Who can account for the supernatural work of our Heavenly Father? Jesus said He would build His Church and the gates of hell would not prevail against it (Matthew 16:18). It seems sometimes that in the areas of the world where there appears to be the least amount of hope, God supernaturally makes a way for people to hear and believe the message.

In many Muslim countries, people see visions in which Jesus appears to them and says, "I am the way." They begin to search for a way to know Him more personally.

In a village in the mountains of Iran, a number of new believers heard that they could find out more about Jesus if they could get the book of the Christians called the Bible. One night, a man had a dream that if he went down to the highway, some men would come by who would be able to give him a Bible.

The next day, he gathered a little offering of money from among the believers in the village, and made his way down the mountainside to the highway that ran through that area. He sat on a rock and began to wait.

Some time later, two men in a car just "happened" to pick up a shipment of Bibles across the border. They were driving along this highway when the steering on their car suddenly locked. They couldn't move it more than an inch.

They finally nudged the steering wheel just enough to get the car over to the side of the road. They got out and put up the hood to figure out what was wrong. A man sitting on a nearby rock called out to them, "Are you the men with the Bibles?"

Stunned that this man should know, they admitted, "Well, yes, we do have Bibles." The old man gave them all the money he had collected, bought as many Bibles as he could, and made his way back to the village.

The men with the Bibles then went back to determine what was wrong with their car but could find nothing. They shrugged their shoulders, got in, and drove away.

They had just been part of a "divine appointment."

■ ■ ■ ■ ■

In the Siberian city of Khabarovsk, a special showing of the "JESUS" film was scheduled for parents and friends of teachers attending an educational conference. Tom Axelson, director of administration and finance for The JESUS Film Project, led the team.

More than 250 people crowded into the Pioneer Palace Theater for the showing. Tom introduced the film, gave some of its background, and told of the great attention given to make sure it was absolutely accurate according to the Scriptures. Nothing unusual.

Jesus' triumphal entry into Jerusalem

Tom slipped out of the auditorium and made his way to a room where the team had stored a supply of Bibles. He spent some time in prayer and then decided to bring down some of the Bibles to distribute to those who would indicate they had received Christ as a result of the showing.

When the film wrapped up, Tom and his interpreter, Zlata Breus, very simply read through the gospel as contained in the *Four Spiritual Laws* booklet. He then led them in a prayer of invitation.

As he concluded his prayer, he indicated that he would meet with those who had prayed to accept the Lord over at the side of the stage. He wanted to give each of them a Bible.

Before he could get off the stage, he was mobbed. The whole audience tried to come at once, most of them weeping. The first lady to come was sobbing uncontrollably. Zlata tried to explain what the woman was saying, but there was too much noise and confusion. Tom sent someone to bring the rest of the Bibles down.

When the crowd was finally gone, Zlata said, "Tom, did you understand what those people were saying?"

Jesus said, "Come to Me, all you who are weary and burdened, and I will give you rest."

"I'm sorry," he said. "I just couldn't make out your words."

"The people were telling me," she said, "that when you were reading the *Four Spiritual Laws* to them, they saw the figure of Jesus from the film standing beside you on the stage. That's why so many of them were sobbing. Jesus had come into their midst."

No Americans were in the audience that night—none to see what had happened. As Tom returned to the hotel, he met a group of people who had been involved in the conference.

"Tell us about the showing," one of them said. "About nine o'clock a few of us got together to pray, because we realized that would be about the time you presented the gospel. We specifically prayed that God would reveal Himself in a special way to those who were there that night."

Tom smiled quietly, "Your prayers were answered—beyond what you would ever believe!"

Zlata recounted some of the numerous conversations with people who had seen the image of Christ standing beside Tom. Then she confessed, "You will never know how meaningful this is to me personally. As a 13-year-old girl, on my summer vacation I met some believers who told me about Jesus, and I accepted Him as my personal Savior.

"When I returned home, I started telling everyone about Him. But my father was a high Communist official, so several times they warned him to shut me up. I continued to talk to people, and the Communists finally said they would send my father to Siberia if I didn't keep quiet. So I stopped talking about Jesus. That was more than forty years ago. In all these years, I have told no one that I believed in Jesus. Not even my husband.

"Tonight is the first time I have spoken for the Lord in all that time. It is more meaningful to me than you can ever know."

No individual, organization, or mission can take any credit for what the Lord is doing in so many parts of the world. It is simply supernatural.

Those who fight against God's power take a grave risk.

A film team made its way to a little Kekchi Indian village in Guatemala. They began to drive around, announcing with their bullhorns that the "JESUS" film would be shown that night. As they drove, they passed a woman cooking something on a fire. She was talking to some Catholic nuns who also had come to the village and had been holding a class nearby.

The woman cooking at the fire suddenly began to curse our Christian team, shouting, "I curse you, and I curse this film!"

The nuns turned to her and said, "You shouldn't curse the film. It is the Word of God, and it is a wonderful film. It tells people how they can live forever, and how they can know Jesus."

A few hours later the woman fell dead by the fire.

Word quickly spread throughout the village that the woman who had cursed the film was dead. People turned out by the hundreds and hundreds to see the film that night. Soon there were more than 1,500. The next night, there were more than 3,500. In two nights of showings, more than a thousand of these people indicated a decision to receive Christ as their personal Savior.

But there is another side of the supernatural. The specter of spiritual warfare arises more often than we sometimes realize.

CHAPTER 15

Victory in
Spiritual Warfare

The young film team in northern Nigeria was determined. The Muslim resistance in Yobe State made it difficult to work there, but Samaylia Mohammed, John Gami, and Daniel Atiyaye would not be deterred. God had called them to help take the gospel to everyone in Nigeria, regardless of whether it was easy and regardless of the reception.

As the hot afternoon sun beat down on the dry, parched soil, the team arrived at the little town of Yadinbuni. A few small churches struggled against the vast Muslim majority. If a public film showing could be done in this place, it certainly would be a great boost to the believers there.

They went to the chief of the town to get permission to show the film in a public place. He was "holding court," as was his custom, lying in a cotton cloth hammock seeking refuge from the sun. Dressed in an elegant, hand-woven, milky-white gari draped over both shoulders, and wearing a tightly-wrapped turban of different colors on his head, he projected quite an impressive appearance. The leaders of his town were seated around him.

"What kind of films do you have?" the chief inquired.

"We have some films about the ancient prophets," Daniel replied. "We have one about Abraham, and one about Isa." Isa is the Muslim pronunciation of Jesus, and the team was hoping that the chief would choose that one. If he didn't, they would show the short film on Abraham first, and wait for an invitation to show the "JESUS" film at a later time.

"I think I would like to see the film about Isa," he replied. "Why don't you show it here in front of my home?"

What a great place for a showing! The chief had built a large pavilion under which hundreds of children in the town were learning to read and write Arabic so they could read the Koran. The pavilion had a permanent roof and open sides. Wooden study benches lined the dirt floor. A fine coating of grit and dust covered every book and piece of paper.

Once the chief had decided on the location, the team went to work setting up the equipment in front of his home. Meanwhile, the chief sent his assistants out to canvass the town and announce the showing.

As darkness fell, the crowd began to swell and the excitement grew quickly. By seven o'clock, nearly three thousand had gathered. The chief's four wives peeked through the doorways of the zaure, the typical entrance room found in large Muslim homes. They were not permitted to attend the showing publicly, but there was no rule against watching the film from the confines of their home.

Daniel started the film and the first thirty-minute reel went just fine. About five minutes into the second reel, however, the picture froze on the screen. Daniel was glad they had been able to bring a back-up projector.

Many of the other teams in the area were not so fortunate. It was never easy showing the film in this territory. A number of the teams reported unusual spiritual warfare. Perhaps it was only unusual to those of us in the West who are sometimes very cynical.

In any event, Daniel lifted the second projector up onto the showing table and proceeded to transfer the reels of film over to it.

The second projector ran for five minutes, and it, too, froze!

Daniel was unsure what to do. He had often repaired projectors in the past. But he could find nothing wrong. He thought it might be the voltage, but the light was bright. Perhaps the belt was ruined. After removing the cover and checking, he knew everything was okay there.

The pastor who was with them suggested they pray. Three of them gathered and laid hands on the motor since the cover had not yet been replaced.

"Oh Lord," Daniel prayed, "we have this great opportunity. We don't know what is wrong with the projector, but we want these people to be able to see this film about Your Son. We don't want them to think that our God is not strong enough to keep the electrical power going at the house of a Muslim chief. Please repair the projector."

As they prayed, the projector began to run again. They were thrilled, and they wrapped up their praying.

As soon as they took their hands off the motor, it stopped again. They quickly put their hands back on the motor and resumed praying and the projector started again. For the remainder of the showing, nearly an hour and a half, the three of them prayed with their hands on the projector.

And three thousand Muslims in northern Nigeria heard the precious story of Jesus.

■ ■ ■ ■ ■ ■

In some countries, the presentation of the film involves supernatural activity with which we are not familiar. When I first began to meet with our film teams in India, I felt uneasy about their ready discussion of encounters with demons and evil spirits. Their stories seemed like something that belonged in horror novels or in a movie like "The Exorcist."

I am now convinced that it is they who live in the "real world." We in the West must learn that there really is a spiritual battle for the souls of men and women.

One afternoon in Bangalore, I met with George Ninan, Charlie Abro, and the Campus Crusade leaders who work under the direction of Thomas Abraham. They told me about the village of Charpandi, in northern India, that was steeped in spirit worship. The village had thirty-one demon worship centers and offered human sacrifices when the local sorcerer ordered it.

Several young men from the tribe had become Christians and had completed the course at the New Life Training Center. They went to this very area to share the message of Christ, and the Lord honored their faith. During the first two months of showing the "JESUS" film and individually sharing Christ with others, 251 people committed their lives to Christ and were baptized.

I talked with several other team leaders about the hard realities of encountering so many witch doctors and other people who are demon-controlled.

"It's not only the people," one of them ventured. "We visit some villages that seem to be totally infested with evil spirits."

"How do you recognize those who are controlled by spirits?" I asked.

"You can see them when you walk through a village. They stare at you with glaring eyes. You can tell that they are extremely angry. They know that our spiritual power is greater than theirs."

I recalled an earlier conversation with the Thailand director, Boonma Panthasri. "We had a showing a few months ago where one of our young technicians tried to cast a demon out of a man. The demon mocked him, and said, 'I know who you are. I know who Jesus is. Don't you know that I am *the strong*? I am *the spirit*. My boss is the spirit leader of the capital. I am the strong village spirit. I am not afraid of you because you don't have enough faith in Jesus Christ.'"

The young man was fearful. He ran back to his team leader, a more mature Christian, shouting, "Please come and help me cast out this spirit."

When the team leader arrived on the scene, the words of the demon were very different. "I know you are all in Jesus Christ," he said. "You are anointed by Jesus Christ. I am afraid and must get out. But remember this, we are working day and night. We will fight against Christians until we have no power."

Having heard enough, the team leader, Sonbat, simply looked into the man's eyes and said, "In the name of the Lord Jesus, I cast you out. You have no right, you have no power to hold this man." Immediately, the spirit left him.

This demon had caused many in the village of Ban Songtun to be sick as a means of maintaining control and instilling fear in them. For many generations, these people had had no defense, no hope, no way of deliverance.

What happened was wonderful. More than half of the villagers indicated decisions to receive Christ, and many who had been sick recovered.

■ □ ■ □ ■ □

The forces of evil are unrelenting, absolutely committed to preventing as many people as possible from hearing the gospel. I was not, however, prepared for the spiritual warfare that would occur in my own life.

I was a skeptic initially. As I talked with film team workers in India, Indonesia, and Thailand, I heard amazing stories of confrontations with the world of the supernatural. At the time, I was gathering reports in preparation for my first book about the "JESUS" film, *I Just Saw JESUS.*

Intellectually, I knew the scriptural passage:

> Our struggle is not against flesh and blood, but against the rulers, against the authorities, against the powers of this dark world and against the spiritual forces of evil in the heavenly realms (Ephesians 6:12).

On a doctrinal level, I believed in the existence of Satan and his legions of demons. But I was unprepared to enter the world of spiritual warfare and demonic attack that was to be a part of my life for the next eighteen months.

In our sophisticated society, mentions of demons are left to the horror thrillers of Stephen King and John Saul. We treat them like science fiction or look at them as the scare tactics of weird, off-the-wall cults. But demons are real. Their power is real.

As Christians, we need have no fear of Satan because "The one who is in you is greater than the one who is in the world" (1 John 4:4). Jesus is still the all-conquering King. He is the King of kings and Lord of lords. One day every knee in heaven and earth and under the earth will bow before Him.

But we must not forget that in today's world we are still in a spiritual battle. It can be fought only with righteousness. To succeed in the battle means to make no compromise with the things of this world. If I cooperate with the enemy in any way, I lose my spiritual power. Without the power of God, I am weak and ineffective. My life needs to be pure and holy before the Lord Jesus Christ.

In January 1984, we made a very important decision. We would take the initiative to show the "JESUS" film in every country of the world, and we would complete the translation of the film into each of the 271 languages spoken by a million or more people. Soon after that, the difficulties began.

Our daughter, Jennifer, who was ten at the time, began having serious health problems, a dangerous asthmatic condition exacerbated by three skin diseases. As the year progressed, her condition deteriorated. Many mornings she woke covered with blood from scratches and broken skin. Despite everything we did, she continued to get worse.

In March, I traveled to India and Indonesia. I listened to the film team workers recount stories of projectors mysteriously blown out, ropes holding up the screens being cut without anyone around, and the appearance of hideous demons at night when they stayed in some of the Buddhist temples. I didn't understand, but I wrote down the stories.

In the months to come, I experienced a series of circumstances far beyond coincidence, much more than simple bad luck. They were, I believe, object lessons by the powers of darkness saying to me, "We'll show you how much power we have and you will regret the day you ever doubted." It began with intensity.

I arrived back from India to find my wonderful, energetic, and spirited wife, Kathy, wrestling with depression and anxiety.

She needed me. Our children needed me. Then my youngest sister called. She was crying. Her husband had just moved out and he was suing for divorce. Hours of late-night phone calls followed, watered with many tears.

And then almost everything started to break.

The carpet began falling apart as if it had rotted. The glass on the thermal-pane door in the back separated and bubbled. The back door latch broke. The neighbor's dog came over and ripped the screens on our back patio. The back fence blew down in a windstorm.

Our new car stopped cold on the highway, its entire electrical system dead. We towed the car to the dealer who had it repaired. Three days later the system went dead again. Then the radio broke. Then the antenna. The seat broke. "It's okay," the mechanics said each time. "Bring it in. We'll repair it."

One 105-degree day in July, in the smog-filled, blistering San Bernardino Valley, during the hottest time of the year, the compressor on the air conditioner in the house went out. Then the television tube burned out and the screen went black. The battery in my watch went dead, as did the batteries in all of our calculators. Despite all of our watering and weeding, the ground cover in the front of the house died from the heat and the smog. As July came to a close, the transmission on the car broke; then the brakes gave out; the tires went flat from mysteriously bent rims; and on and on.

While my car was in the garage, one day I drove Kathy's car down the winding mountain road from the Arrowhead Springs Conference Center. As I rounded a curve, a huge rock dropped off the cliff onto my windshield. The entire windshield shattered and dropped into my lap. I slammed on the brakes and managed to get the car over to the side of the road. My heart was racing. Was someone trying to kill me? The "crack" had been so loud that at first I thought someone was shooting at me.

I could see no one up on the cliff. I carefully lifted the glass off my lap and climbed out the door shaking the splinters onto the roadside gravel.

"Thank You, Lord," I breathed. "Once again, You have protected me. I love You."

I got back in the car and drove to the garage.

At this point, I was still not aware that anything out of the ordinary was happening. Bad things happen to a lot of people. I wasn't the type of person who saw Satan behind every bush. We had just gone through a pretty tough summer, but so had other people. We would simply have to keep going, try to pay the bills, and wait for the Lord's solution.

At that time I didn't keep track of the things that went wrong. No reason to, really. It wasn't until a few months later that I began to look back and list the incredible events. And things continued to happen.

When summer ended, I went to visit our film teams in West Africa. While I was in Mali, my suitcase was stolen with all of my clothing.

In October, things got even worse. Four of our personal financial supporters wrote us that, for a variety of reasons, they could no longer help us. In the middle of all the other problems, we suddenly faced the loss of $400 a month. But our financial difficulties were only beginning.

By the first of December we had more than $10,000 in medical bills and car and home repairs. There was no let-up. The weather turned very cold in California and our heater wouldn't start. Our mailbox was smashed by vandals and the stamps taken off the

letters. The batteries in all the calculators went dead again. The
chain on the power lawn mower snapped. The radio in Kathy's
car broke. My watch crystal shattered. One day I went into our den
to relax by playing a few praise songs on my guitar. I discovered
that the entire bridge had come off my guitar and had wrapped
up in a ball with the strings.

Four days later as I came up the front walk of my home, a
vulture swooped down and dropped a dead rabbit at my feet.

The attacks were now becoming more personal. Four days
earlier I could have been killed in the collapse of the smashed
windshield. Now, here was another omen of death, delivered
almost as a warning. This was more than going through a "bad
time." This was a taunt by the forces of evil. It was not a battle I
wanted to be in. I had not set myself up as some kind of "exorcist."

In the past, when I had heard stories of people who cast out
demons or were involved with demon-possessed people, I had
always listened. The stories were always interesting. Some I believed; some I was pretty sure were exaggerated. Mostly, they were
not things I wanted to be involved with. They were for people
from religious traditions other than my own.

But now I realized I had to do something. So I did the only
thing I knew to do. I prayed. "Lord, I claim the power and
protection of the blood of Christ. I thank You that in the midst of
all these circumstances we can still trust You. We will do that. We
will trust You." This was my daily prayer. I knew the Lord's
command to "give thanks in every circumstance," and I wanted to
be obedient to that. But sometimes it was tough.

As the new year opened, nothing changed. In January the
wind blew away our garbage cans. The toilet overflowed, soaking
and staining the rugs. My electric razor quit working. The car air
conditioner and the speedometer broke.

During the next year, more than sixty-five things broke. We
bought a new car; someone hit it. We moved to a new house; it
was flooded by a broken pipe. Our children got sick—Jennifer
with a life-threatening virus that caused thousands of sores to
break out over her body.

The harassment continued for eighteen months.

I shared what was happening with a number of leaders in our organization. They laid hands on me and prayed for God's deliverance. Nothing changed.

I began to search through all the artifacts I had ever brought back from any foreign country. Was it possible that some demons had attached themselves in some way to one of these objects? I didn't know. I found a little rubber statue of a native from Borneo. I destroyed it. I even threw out the tea I had bought in Sri Lanka.

I invited our pastor to come and pray over our home. I asked him to place his hands on our cars and plead the blood of Christ over our vehicles. He did.

A very close friend of our family said it was obvious to her that we had been cursed. She sent me a prayer to pray to help deal with curses. I walked around our home and prayed this prayer aloud.

During the next several months the incidents continued to occur, but not in such great volume. Then suddenly, after eighteen months, they stopped. I don't know why. I suppose someone who is a greater theologian than myself would know the reason. I don't know which of the things we did was responsible. Maybe all of them. Maybe none of them. Perhaps if we did know, we would try to reduce it to some formula for how to deal with Satan and his legions, and lose track of our total, utter, complete dependence upon our wonderful, risen Lord Jesus.

I also know that many people still pray for me, our family, and the ministry of The JESUS Film Project. In the quiet of my own heart, I feel that those prayers somehow move the hands of God to "bind the strong man" in our lives and to allow our ministry through the "JESUS" film to continue once again without as much opposition.

What I have shared here is only a glimpse of the spiritual warfare going on in many lives and in many places. The more the "JESUS" film moves into new territories, the more spiritual opposition there is likely to be. I know of no person who is a part of this project who has not been tested in many ways. Certainly, those young men who have gone to the remote jungles to record new languages have faced it more than others.

We can be assured of this: As long as we invade the strongholds of evil with the life-changing message of the King, the devil and his legions will do whatever they can to stop the effort. We must again draw on the truth of Ephesians 6:12: "Our struggle is not against flesh and blood, but against the rulers, against the authorities, against the powers of this dark world and against the spiritual forces of evil in the heavenly realms."

What is the lesson? That we might never serve our God in our own strength. The greatest fear I have is that I might attempt to do God's work in my own power. I am afraid, desperately afraid, that I might begin to believe that my own plans and strategies could accomplish His purposes. Without the continual touch of Jesus, we labor in the evangelistic enterprise with an empty, hollow message and with shallow lives of self-effort robbed of the powerful energy of the life-giving Spirit.

With Him, all things are possible. We can storm the strongholds of Satan. We can snatch the hearts of men and women from his snares. And with the victorious cross of Christ before us, we can deliver them to their eternal destiny in the loving, forgiving, and protecting family of God.

Nowhere was the mission more important than in our next goal, the heartbreaking country of Cambodia.

CHAPTER 16

The "Killing Fields"

Nine thousand skulls, piled seventy feet high. Shelf after shelf of sun-bleached bones—men, women, babies.

I stood by the Killing Fields Memorial just outside of Phnom Penh, the capital city of Cambodia, and recalled the nightmare. One and a half million people, perhaps more, slaughtered with a viciousness unknown in modern history. A little nation of eight million torn apart by the murderous Pol Pot in a four-year reign of terror.

I walked on narrow dikes between the excavated grave sites. At the bottom of each pit were bones. On the pathways, on the sides of pits, everywhere—the bones of the tortured victims. I looked down at my feet and saw three teeth in the dirt.

Was life so cheap that there could not even be enough time or money to give all these victims a decent burial? And how many still lay under rice paddies, their bodies never discovered? In fact, the government had halted the excavations. There were acres and acres of mass grave sites here, and at least two hundred more sites just like this one in other parts of the country. For what purpose should all the bodies be unearthed? Who was still alive to care?

I looked at a sign placed in a pit under a tree: "151 women and children found buried here. Most of them were naked." Our guide said the enemy had chosen the pit near the tree, so they could save bullets by smashing the heads of the babies against the tree and tossing them into the grave.

Another sign said, "162 bodies without heads found here." And in pit after pit we read the grim statistics of those who had perished.

The horror of one and a half million Cambodians killed by the Khmer Rouge will never be forgotten.

At the central monument, the guard opened the doors and I put my hands on the skulls. These were young men and women, 16 to 20 years old. Their lives were just beginning. Did they have a chance to hear the message of Christ before they died? Probably not.

I wondered again, *Why don't I have a greater sense of urgency for spreading the gospel? In how many places does the inhumanity of man without God result in thousands of people being killed every day? Hundreds of little wars go on in so many places. What can one person do, anyway?*

I can't do everything, I concluded, *but I must do something. I need to keep trying in every way possible to make sure everyone in the world gets at least one chance to hear the message of Jesus and feel His divine touch.*

It was hot and humid. In the still, sultry oppression of the afternoon, I imagined the fields before me. On a day, perhaps much like this one, beaten, tortured men and women had been forced to dig their own graves. As sweat poured off their naked bodies, Khmer Rouge soldiers sadistically beat their backs until the flesh was raw and blood streamed down their legs.

The "Killing Fields" are a stark reminder of how much the world needs the peace of Jesus.

And then the final blows came, accentuating the torture. Anguished cries of terror and mind-screaming pain going on and on as a dull hoe was used to chop the heads from the dying victims. And soon, the dark blackness of the blood would soak the grimy, ragged clothing, and the lifeless forms would be pushed atop the pile of skeletons in the bottom of the pit.

The next afternoon we visited the special prison of torture where the educated people of the city were brought to "confess." Of the twenty thousand men, women, and children brought to the prison, only seven people lived through the ordeal. The prison was a three-story high-school building commandeered by the Khmer Rouge for one of the most horrific houses of pain ever devised.

In one wing, the most famous of the prisoners were chained to beds and killed by cutting their throats when they could no longer invent anything else to confess. Their emaciated bodies, like stick-figures inside a pile of greasy rags, awaited the final slash of the knives across their throats.

As we walked in and out of the rooms, we saw the floors blackened by bloodstains. On the walls hung blurring photos, taken on the day of liberation, of the slaughtered bodies.

In another wing, each classroom had been cut into ten or more little cells where prisoners were chained day and night, their very existence a living hell. One bowl of rice a day. A shower every two weeks. And unending days and nights of torture. Stretching racks. Hanging beams. Pots of water to progressively drown victims. Vises to clamp the arms as they pulled out the fingernails and cut the fingers off—an inch at a time. And other unspeakable tortures designed for women that sent shudders of disbelief through my body.

In another wing, barbed wire covered every balcony to keep prisoners from diving onto the concrete below to end their pain quickly in suicide.

And on the walls again, pictures of the thousands who had died there. Eight or ten were from other countries—America, France, Australia, Germany. But most were young Cambodian families, including thousands of children. The objective was to kill every child so there would be no revenge at a later date.

We even saw photos of those who had done the killing. Most were young. Many appeared to be teenagers. Most were still alive. They had never been captured and brought to justice.

Then I had an incredible thought: *God will still forgive these killers if they will acknowledge their sins.* He is willing to forgive even these gross human atrocities if the guilty persons would turn to Him. The Scriptures say that God's kind of love surpasses the ability of mortal men to comprehend. I believe it.

Yes, the Lord would want them brought to justice. And yes, they should pay in this life for their terrible deeds. But in the end, His grace is unlimited and His forgiveness to those who repent is unending.

That night a small group of business leaders with whom I had been traveling gathered to hear from the Campus Crusade for Christ director in Cambodia. I introduced Vek Huong Taing and his wife, Samouen, to our group.

"I want you to meet a couple tonight," I began, "who I consider to be real heroes of the faith. Their dedication to our Lord and to His Great Commission is beyond anything I have ever known.

"A few days before the collapse of Cambodia, Dr. Bailey Marks, director of the Campus Crusade ministry in Asia, sent a telex to Huong here in Phnom Penh. He asked him if he would like to be evacuated, in light of the daily newspaper reports that Phnom Penh was likely to fall.

Vek Huong and Samouen Taing direct the film ministry in Cambodia.

"Huong replied a few days later, 'We have decided to serve our Lord Jesus Christ by working toward reaching Cambodia for Him until the last minute of our lives.' Ten days later the city fell. Every person was ordered by the Khmer Rouge to leave the city.

"Huong and Samouen, with their 2½-month-old baby, began the trek out of the city," I continued. "We did not hear from them for four years. I want you to hear a little of what happened during that time."

Huong stood to speak. He was short and thin. With his quiet voice and his glasses, he might be mistaken for a researcher in a dusty laboratory. But when he began to tell his story, we felt we were in the presence of a spiritual giant—like one of those heroes of the past we wish we could have met. Now we were awestruck by the accounts of how God spared his life.

"My father was one of the first people introduced to Christ by the missionaries fifty years ago," he began. "We had ten brothers and sisters in our family. Six of them were killed by the Khmer Rouge. One was my sister, whose picture, along with her five children, you saw on the wall in the prison this afternoon. They were killed in that place."

For the next hour he recounted the agonies of walking across the country with his wife and little baby trying to escape the Communist-backed Khmer Rouge. He climbed coconut trees to get food for the soldiers. Sometimes they would let him keep a coconut. But most of the time, he and his family were near death from starvation.

He told us of praying that God would spare their lives. "But," he said, "we were willing to die for our Lord." One day he went fishing in a little rice paddy. The water was not deep, but he caught a fish almost a foot long. And he caught one fish there every day for the next thirty days.

As the days turned into months, the time for their wedding anniversary came. Huong could see no possible way to celebrate. But Samouen was insistent.

"Take these baby clothes," she urged, "and see if you can trade them for some extra food."

Huong found a man with four freshly killed rats, but the man was unwilling to give them up. Finally he relented and said Huong could have the heads and the skin. So he butchered the rats, keeping the good plump bodies to cook, and gave Huong the heads and skin. Huong took them home to his wife. She boiled them and made a rat soup to have with their rice that night.

Samouen picked up the story. "We were so hungry," she recalled, "that we were even grateful for those rat heads. That night as my husband held me, we talked about what we should do when the Communists finally came for us and separated us from each other. My husband told me not to cry. 'Remember,' he said, 'we will be going to heaven and all of our pain will be over.' And so we made an agreement that we would not be sad when it came time for us to be separated and killed."

Through a dramatic series of miracles, they made it into a refugee camp in Thailand. There, a Reuters reporter from England interviewed them and Huong's name went across the wires. A sharp Transworld Radio broadcaster in Guam picked it up, and she immediately called our Central Asian Office in the Philippines to inform Bailey Marks.

Within days, permission had been granted for the couple's release, and they were on their way to America.

"Our little boy had never slept in a bed," Samouen smiled at us. "We had told him, since he was old enough to understand, that our Lord had everything and He would take care of us. So when he saw this bed, he asked if that was the bed of our Lord. We told him that our Lord had given this bed for us to sleep in. He was so excited.

"He had never seen shoes before. The first time he went to a shoe store though, he didn't want us to buy sandals. He wanted some big leather shoes that squeaked when he walked. When he and his father left the camp to go to Bangkok, he saw his first car. He immediately asked, 'Does our Lord have a car? Can we ask Him for one?' We did ask Him for one, and He provided it for us to use during our first days in the United States.

"But Cambodia is our home. We will continue to serve here. We both have many sad memories here. My parents and Huong's mother were killed by the Khmer Rouge. God gave us back our lives so that we could serve Him, so that we could reach Cambodia for Christ. This is our second life."

Even as she spoke, the Khmer Rouge were still vying for power. That the world community would even permit them to come back into any type of power-sharing arrangement seemed incredible. Some people believe that the persecution could happen again. And if it does, certainly those who take a strong stand for the kingdom of God will be the first targeted for death.

But the Cambodian Christians are standing strong for their faith. That morning I had gone out to one of the branches of the Mekong River to witness the baptism of 136 new believers. Pastors from seventeen little churches came to baptize those from their own congregations who were making their public professions of faith.

I talked with one of the pastors. He had conducted a film showing near his church just four days before. "This is a wonderful day," he enthused. "On Wednesday night we showed the 'JESUS' film and about four hundred people came. A large number wanted to place their faith in Christ. On Thursday night

Pastors from seventeen churches baptize 136 new believers in the Mekong River.

we had our first follow-up meeting to help confirm many in the faith who had made their decisions the night before.

"On Friday night we began the six-week follow-up Bible study. And today I will baptize thirteen of those who trusted the Lord as their personal Savior on Wednesday night."

It was an awesome sight. A choir on the banks sang "Amazing Grace," and 136 candidates walked into the water. One by one they were asked, "Do you trust Jesus Christ as your personal Savior and Lord? Do you determine to follow only Him for the rest of your life and to turn away from all other gods?" All responded, "Yes!"

"Then I baptize you in the name of the Father, the Son, and the Holy Spirit. Amen."

In Cambodia, as in other countries of the world, the blood of the martyrs is precious to the Lord. The church continues to grow here in the shadows of the "Killing Fields." And the examples of the believers in Cambodia have led other disciples of our Lord to a new level of commitment.

But sometimes the price of that commitment is extremely high.

CHAPTER 17

A Price to Pay

If there were a Hall of Fame in world evangelism, many of the "JESUS" film team workers would be enshrined. No one will ever know the selfless dedication and sacrifice of these team members. Few Western Christians would be willing to pay the price these men have paid for the advancement of the gospel.

One of these is John Eluru. He paid the ultimate price.

It happened during the recording of the Ateso language for a tribe in the country of Uganda. The technicians had finished the first week of recording and had gone to pick up more people from the village and bring them into the city where the recording was going on. As they were returning to the city, a band of guerilla fighters burst out from the side of the road and began to riddle the truck with automatic weapons fire.

They shot one of the men in the head, killing him instantly. A little girl was shot in the leg, and the man who had played the part of Jesus, John Eluru, was shot through the heart. One of the tires was hit, but the driver kept going anyway. They drove more than a mile-and-a-half on just the rim of the wheel, just barely managing to escape from the guerilla fighters.

When they realized they were going to make it, they headed for the hospital. The little girl was rushed into the emergency room along with John, and the man who had been killed was taken to the morgue.

That night as John lay dying, our film technician, Abraham Kasika, went in to see him. John raised up a little on one elbow, obviously in excruciating pain. He turned slightly and said weakly, "Abraham, don't stop the dubbing. Uganda needs this film. I have done my part, but don't stop the work, and don't ever be afraid."

The next morning John Eluru died. Today he's with the Lord, and I imagine that he is looking down over the battlements of heaven with great joy. Every time the completed Ateso film is shown in Uganda, the voice of John Eluru as Jesus tells hundreds of his own people how to know God.

The film in the Ateso language first showed in the high school where John had been the principal. The day it was shown, his voice, playing the character of Jesus, helped scores of young men and women in that school come to know Jesus in a personal way. He could have left no finer legacy to his students.

Although John Eluru is dead, his voice lives on in the "JESUS" film, and many more thousands will come to know the Savior because of him.

One day, as I met with the incredible team of engineers and administrators from our Master Dubbing Studio, I wondered why the production of every "JESUS" film translation is filled with such difficulty and trial. The discussion had turned to the problems encountered.

"What's the toughest thing about doing this job?" I asked.

"Finding the right people to trust," one replied. "We don't speak any of these languages, so we are completely dependent on the missionaries and helpers in the various countries to be sure that the film is being translated accurately and delivered correctly."

"I think the toughest thing for me," one of the other technicians admitted, "is to go back to a country and re-dub long parts of the film because it's not right—even though we worked really hard on it the first time." I knew they had just finished the fourth dubbing of the Uyghar language. This was for an unreached group of Muslims who lived on the border of southern Russia and northern China—seven million people, with no church and very few known believers. And these men, trying to dub a film on the life of Jesus, were working with atheistic Communist Party members in southern Russia. It had to be difficult.

But another battle, an unseen one, also was being fought against the "rulers and princes of the powers of darkness" who would not be pleased that another stronghold was falling to Christ. If we were going to invade the territory of the enemy continually, we would have to expect opposition.

The letters from the dubbing teams in the field told the story even more graphically. I pulled out the letter we had just received from Willie Erasmus, then a field technician in Malawi, Africa, addressed to Ron Green, the director of our Master Studio:

Dear Ron,

I am dispatching with this letter the tapes for the Yao language. This was, by far, the most challenging recording we have done. Given the fact that this language will be used predominantly among Muslims, we can understand the spiritual attacks. I want to update you on the sequence of events.

About 30 kilometers outside Livingstone, on my way to Lusaka, Zambia, I found a man in the middle of the road walking toward me. I blew the horn anticipating he would leave the road as all do in such circumstances, but this man kept coming. When I swerved to pass him on the left, he veered to the left. I then adjusted to pass him on the right, and he veered to the right. It looked as if he was going to jump in front of the vehicle. I thought he was intoxicated and moved over more to the right, but he jumped toward the van.

He had an axe in his left hand, with which he lashed out toward the windshield. The blow ricocheted off the left front-door pillar smashing the vent window, the door window, and the left rear-view mirror. The glass flew all over the cab and cut my hands. I praise the Lord that Marie was not with me as she would have been badly cut sitting in the passenger seat. When I reported the incident to the police, they said they knew about this man. He is mentally disturbed, and they are trying to catch him.

When I came out of the police station, I had a flat tire, which turned out later to be from the rim being cracked. The tire, being tubeless, could not hold air. The man at the repair shop said he had never seen such a thing happen before, especially when it was obvious that the wheel had not hit any rock and was not damaged where the crack was.

When I reached the border, the Malawi customs did not allow me into the country, saying I needed a special government clearance. We had applied for this but were told that since I was not going to do any public speaking, I would not need the special clearance.

I then had to return to Chipata in Zambia, and I slept in the van at the police station. The following day at 12, Marie and Crispin Gondwe, our director in Malawi, arrived with the clearance, and they let me in.

The following day I came down with a terrible fever and was in bed for a day. We prayed and the fever was gone that evening.

We started the recording one day late, and suddenly, for no apparent reason, the sound just disappeared in the middle of a loop-take. We checked everything—connections, wires, cables, and microphone. We could find nothing that could have caused the breakdown. We prayed and engaged in spiritual warfare. Soon after this, the sound was back, and we could continue with the recording.

Then a day or two later the tape was damaged. We had been recording for a couple of hours. When we got to this loop, the tape looked as if it had been pinched by the recorder. We discontinued using the rest of this tape.

Then we had a battle with one loop where we could not erase a sound that we found at the beginning. I tried to save the previous loop because the character had already left and was not available any more. In this effort, I hit the "Record" button. I could not believe that I did this, but I did, and once more we erased a couple of seconds of the picture as well as the recording.

During the "Jesus" part, and around the crucifixion and resurrection, we had three power failures, some lasting up to four or five hours.

As for the voices, they were mostly imported from the Yao-speaking region some 240 kilometers away from Blantyre. The Yao language is forbidden to be taught in the schools. In Malawi, only two languages can be taught in private and government schools: the official language—Chichewa—and English. So, very few people can read Yao. We had a big problem finding enough people who could read Yao and who are fluent Yao speakers without a Chichewa accent.

We especially found it difficult with the older voices. With the women, this problem was exceptionally challenging. We worked 1½ hours on the part of Elizabeth.

We were very blessed with the narrator. Although he had a younger voice than we would have preferred, he was an excellent reader and did this part very well.

The Yao language, we found, was one-and-a-half to two times longer than English. We would find words like *yiwalijiganyisye,* which means *taught* in English. Or, *jwakutyotchela,* which means *from* in English. This was particularly challenging when we did the lip-synch loops. Although the seconds allotted seemed fine during the video-fit exercise, it turned out not to fit when we did the lip-synch with pauses and breath breaks.

But God was working and we were just amazed to see how He once more intervened and took control of the situation.

After we had done the auditions, there were still a couple of voices that we did not have. One was the voice of Jesus. We prayed earnestly that God would provide the right man for this part. The missionaries in Blantyre all knew about the recording and were all praying with us. One met a man who was a Yao speaker and sent him over to audition. He turned out to be a God-sent man, the right man for the role. He was a committed Christian who grew up among the Yao of Mozambique and had a vision of returning to Mozambique to do mission work among the Yao-speaking community. Mozambique has no Christian churches or missionaries working among the Yao speakers.

All in all, we had a great time and we are looking forward to the premiere as well as conducting the "JESUS" film training for many mission groups who wish to work with this film when it is completed.

We just got word from Pretoria that our house was burglarized. We don't know yet what was stolen.

Three mission families who were living up in the Mangochi area were so terrorized by the Muslim community that two moved away. One went back to the U.S. and one to Blantyre. The third couple stayed on, but was bewitched. Very strange things began happening to them, their children, and their property. After the wife fell ill and the doctors could not diagnose the illness, they, too, returned home to the U.S. We are praying for them. All of this has just shown us the incredible spiritual warfare that we are engaged in.

We can thus expect to see great miracles happen with the Yao film. We hope to start Ndebele the 20th of October.

Please send our love to all and special greetings to Chris.

Yours in Christ,
Willie Erasmus

I looked at the letter again and thanked the Lord once more for allowing me to work with this wonderful team of engineers, programmers, administrators, and technicians.

The Lord had originally sent Pierce Barnes and his wife, Lee. Pierce had developed the computerized dialogue replacement process and the most effective portable dubbing equipment available in the world. Hollywood had never developed the art of portable dubbing, because they couldn't make enough money dubbing films into Swahili and Shona.

One night I asked Jack Valenti, president of the Motion Picture Association of America, what the most-dubbed film in the world was.

"Gone With the Wind," he replied.

"How many languages?" I inquired.

"About thirty."

As of 2002, the total language translations of the "JESUS" film have already passed 750, making it the most translated film in the history of the motion picture industry. Those who deserve the thanks are the men and women of the Master Studio operation where the primary technical work is done.

Ron and Carol Green direct a crew of talented, dedicated people. Tom Dennen, Irv Klaschus, Jim Witmer, and Chris Hayes have led the way with the engineering and programming design. Les Kisling, Mike Milchling, and Kary Hagen bear the brunt of the editing and mixing. Out on the field, Joel Haley, David Reeves, Greg Riggs, and a host of others are making yet another foray to record new translations of the film.

In the Orlando Master Studio, Tom Dennen mixes the music and sound effects with the newly recorded voice tracks to produce a new language translation.

I always find the process fascinating. The first step is to locate the financing. It costs 35,000 dollars to record and edit each language. We decided early in the growth of The JESUS Film Project that we would not initiate a project until the funds were in. I always hated appeals where you were asked to fund a deficit, or if you didn't give now, something would collapse. So we just decided that we wouldn't record a language or launch a team until the Lord impressed a church or an individual to provide the funds.

The next steps are to find someone to do the written translation of the script and recruit someone to be the dialogue director. He makes sure the blind man delivers the lines with great emotion when he says, "I can see! I can see!" Those doing the written translation turn to the translation of the Bible as their beginning point. For the written translation, we usually look for a national Christian like a university professor, or sometimes a Wycliffe translator. I am tremendously grateful for the work of Wycliffe Bible Translators and others who have gone before us into many areas to work on the translations of the Scriptures. We can do the film translation so much more easily if they have already finished the Gospel of Luke.

To that end, we are partnering with The Seed Company of Wycliffe in order to translate the Gospel of Luke and the "JESUS" film script for thirty of the world's largest unreached people groups. This is a terrific example of the Body of Christ working together to accelerate the spread of the gospel.

One time we were translating the film into the Zhuang language for a people group living in southern China and northern Vietnam. Few believers were available to help, and the Bible had not yet been translated. We finished our translation of the film and took it to one of those believers to have it checked.

He said, "You did pretty well, except for this one place. You translated *angels* as *fairies*." We quickly changed that. We praise God for the Bible translation ministries. We need them. In fact, I believe God planned for us to work together as Christian organizations far more than we do.

The script is translated from the English original so that, ideally, each line can be spoken in the same length of time as the original. The translator then counts the syllables to make sure the new words will fit. Any lines too long or too short are changed to

These Tulu speakers in India gather to record a crowd scene.

suitable lines with the same meaning. This is a very delicate process. Since 70 percent of the script is taken from the Gospel of Luke, it means we are editing Scripture. Every care is taken to ensure that the meaning is not lost in any situation.

After the new language script is finished, the translator watches the film and reads the translation aloud, double-checking that the new script fits with the existing video.

Then it is time to record. The dialogue director auditions many voices. There are forty-two speaking parts and more than 3,000 individual lines to be recorded. The director looks for people who have had some acting experience. Even the most remote tribes likely have conducted some kinds of plays.

Each speaker is then assigned a time of day to report to record his lines. From past experience, we know approximately how long it will take to record each part. It may range from ten or fifteen minutes for the part of the angel to three or four days for the part of Jesus.

A recording session in Zimbabwe results in a new translation of "JESUS" in the Shona language.

When it is time to begin, the new language speaker watches the video of the "JESUS" film repeating one line over and over. He will then record the line again and again until it fits the movement of lips as closely as possible. It takes about two long weeks of work to record all the lines.

The recordings are then sent back to our Master Studio where each word or phrase in each line is carefully lip-synchronized with the "JESUS" film images. This takes another two weeks to complete.

To complete the soundtrack, David Reeves synchronizes the visual and audio portions of a new language version.

Next, the lip-synched voices are adjusted for things like volume and echoing, and mixed with the sound effects to make the final soundtrack.

The soundtrack is then sent off as a videotape "check copy" to the national church or approval committee. They make sure that all the words are correct and that this translation will communicate to the intended audience.

If everything is okay and no corrections are needed, the final videotape masters are produced and the first 16mm or 35mm film prints are made for distribution.

It is a grueling process, never easy. And it has to be precise. It's the Word of God brought to life on the screen. If it is done right, people will respond. Not because of the technical job we have done, but because of the power of His words.

It is the transforming words of Jesus that move these young engineers to give their lives and abilities for the cause of the kingdom. It was the motivation for John Eluru to risk his life. And it was the love of Jesus that led Romulo Sauñe to give his life for his Savior.

As the Spanish "JESUS" film came to Peru, Romulo knew it would have to be translated into the Quechua dialect to reach the Indians living in Ayacucho. God used this man to translate the Ayacucho Quechua Bible. So he became the voice to narrate the "JESUS" film in that language.

But because of his vibrant witness for the Lord, he was a marked man by the Shining Path guerrillas of Peru.

One bright Saturday afternoon in September, Romulo—along with his brother, nephew, and cousin—and several other Christians were suddenly stopped on a winding section of Los Liberatadores Road by members of the Shining Path. They were just ten miles from home. The rebels forced all the passengers to leave their vehicles and lined the men up along the side of the road. Machine gun fire burst forth and Romulo and his relatives were killed instantly.

Enrique Sauñe, father of both Romulo and Rubin, watched his sons die. He said his sons knew what was going to happen, and they bowed their heads and commended their spirits to God. By the time the army personnel arrived to stop the bloodshed, seven other civilians and two policemen also had been killed.

The news of the death of this great Quechua leader and his loved ones spread rapidly from church to church and village to village. Three days later, in spite of threats and warnings by guerrillas, more than 2,500 believers formed a triumphant two-mile-long funeral procession crossing the city. Thousands of other Ayacuchos of all faiths and persuasions lined the streets and the main plaza as a sign of respect. Worship and praise through testimony and song continued from early in the morning until late afternoon.

The father of one of the victims said to the guerrillas in his funeral message: "I want to tell you that God loves you. Give your life to Him. I want you to know that I have already forgiven you, for God has also forgiven me."

In its four hundred years of existence, the ancient colonial city of Ayacucho had never seen a funeral service of this magnitude.

■ ■ ■ ■ ■

In the summer of 1994, the world was shaken by the scenes of thousands dying in Rwanda. In the factional fighting between Tutsis and Hutus, the people had no safe place to go to. Many fled to Zaire and died in a cholera epidemic. We prayed for the safety and protection of our three film teams.

Despite the chaos, team workers kept showing the film as they retreated toward the borders. The worse things got, the more responsive people were to the gospel. On July 25, Helen Hoeksema, my assistant, brought me the telex that said some of our team members had been killed.

The national materials coordinator, Mrs. Marie Umuhire, responsible for the translation and distribution of all the follow-up literature for the teams, was killed along with her husband, a guard, and all of their children.

These men and women, and many others, join the heroes of Hebrews chapter 11. Perhaps from their position in the heavenlies, Romulo Sauñe, John Eluru, and the Rwandan film team workers will be cheering us on as we keep taking the gospel to those who have never heard.

But what about those who have heard? What about those who live in our own country, where the gospel can be heard at almost any time of any day or night? What about our own state, our city, and those who live right next door? Or possibly even within our own homes?

CHAPTER 18

Saturating America With "JESUS"

W e live with the danger that while trying to reach the world with the gospel of Christ, we'll walk right past our neighbors.

Every morning when I drive up Hancock Street where I live, I think about my neighbors, their problems, and the pressures they face. And I realize again that I have a responsibility to reach out not only to the "uttermost parts of the earth" spoken of in the Scriptures, but also to those who live in my own neighborhood, city, and country.

In the midst of great material wealth for many in this country, we struggle to keep our marriages, families, and relationships together. We are the most promoted-to, advertised-to, media-saturated, information-overloaded society in history. In the thick of it all, we sometimes lose perspective on what is really important. The quiet, spiritual parts of our lives are drowned out by the din of shrieking advertisements that demand we buy more, more, more.

Yet, even within this media blitz, the "JESUS" film speaks to our own society. It offers peace in the middle of chaos, and hope in the depths of suffering. And for those who have moved here from other countries, the "JESUS" film often provides the first opportunity for them to hear the message of Christ in their own language.

When we moved to our little community in Southern California, I immediately started searching for those who looked or spoke as if they might have immigrated here from another area of the world. The people at the donut shop were from Cambodia. The man at the laundry was from India. The women at my wife's

Families throughout the United States are receiving a gift of the "JESUS" video from churches in their city.

nail-care shop were from Vietnam. My barber was from Slovakia. The waiters at the restaurant were from Iran, and the workers who cleaned the offices at night were from Bolivia.

We gave videocassettes of the "JESUS" film, in their own individual languages, to them at Christmas time. They were grateful. They all watched. Not all have received the Lord yet, but they have had a chance to hear and see the story of Christ in their own mother tongue.

As we begin a new century, the Lord has seen fit to accelerate organized use of the "JESUS" video to help reach those who have not yet responded to the Savior. A massive campaign to give a "JESUS" video to every home in America is now under way. The idea, initiated in Australia, has developed in a marvelous, creative way through the efforts of Marvin Kehler, director of Campus Crusade for Christ in Canada. They distributed more than 193,000 videos in the first two years of their outreach.

It's a quiet campaign in many ways: no big-name speakers, and no traffic jams or masses packing out a stadium. Called the JESUS Video Project, it mobilizes battalions of volunteers in communities across America who work in teams of two. For many of them, the strategy takes the fear out of witnessing.

"The 'JESUS' video allows you to extend your heart and your hand and the gospel in a non-threatening and rewarding way," one woman participant told the NBC news crew who were covering the story for national television.

It begins with prayer, coupled with training local volunteers under the supervision of a local committee and pastors. Preceding the distribution, church members go door-to-door, leaving door-hangers that tell of the upcoming free video offer.

It says:

There are two best-selling films about extraterrestrials.
This one is true.

When the video is delivered to the door, volunteers ask the residents if they can come back in a few weeks to take a six-question survey. Most agree. Within a few weeks of delivering the "JESUS" video, a volunteer returns to complete the brief questionnaire. That's when they hear the wonderful responses.

One teacher in Austin, Texas, gave the video to the mother of one of her students. When the family of seven watched it, all seven received Christ. They now attend church and have shown the video to many of their neighbors.

In Homeworth, Ohio, Phil Norcom, who owns a plant nursery, coordinated the "JESUS" video distribution in his church. Each of the first two houses where he left the video had a teenage boy. Both trusted Christ. Each then introduced a friend to Phil; both friends wanted to know the Savior.

In fact, participating churches report seeing at least 16 percent of those watching the "JESUS" video indicate a decision for Christ.

With more than 750 language versions of "JESUS" currently available on video, the plan translates easily for other countries, as well as serving diverse ethnic groups within our communities. A Korean church in Colorado, for example, ordered six hundred "JESUS" videos in the Korean language for their part in the area-wide outreach.

Often the multiplication goes far beyond the efforts of the volunteers. One worker in Winnipeg, Manitoba, returned to do the survey with a family who lived a block from the church. Three

of them indicated a decision for Christ. That family gave the
"JESUS" video to a relative whose family then watched it. The
whole family wanted to know Christ. They then passed it on to a
third family. In all, the volunteer reported, thirteen people in
three families indicated a commitment to the Savior.

One benefit, many pastors reported, is the less threatening
form of evangelism the strategy offers, both for the recipient and
the church member. Texas pastor Harland Merriman told of one
woman in his congregation who came back to say, "If this is
evangelism, I wish I had been doing it for twenty years!"

As we reach our own country, our own area, with the message
of Christ, we have a chance to influence the world. And this is
happening. Back in Russia, distribution of the film was beginning
to accelerate.

CHAPTER 19

Return to Russia

As the news of the "JESUS" film began to spread, thousands of Christians in more than two hundred countries began to request copies. National pastors, Christian workers, missionaries, and laymen offered to give their time to show the film if we could provide them with a 16mm copy of the film and a projector.

Because of the generosity of churches and individuals, more than fourteen thousand films and four thousand projectors had been shipped out to various countries by 2002. Video sales had topped a million and were climbing rapidly. But what happened to these projectors once they reached the field?

Two years after he received his projector, I met Mikhail Savin at a conference. He was a tall Russian pastor from Krasnodar with an unruly thatch of graying hair. He spoke no English, but his enthusiasm and the twinkle in his eyes were evident as he spoke through our interpreter.

"Tell me what has happened since you received your projector two years ago," I asked.

He smiled. "I and the churches in my area have shown the film more than a thousand times.

"There are four churches in Krasnodar who work together," he explained. "We decided there should be no day when the film and projector were not used."

"What kind of places do you show the film?" I wondered.

"Any kind you can think of," he smiled, "prisons, factories, schools, 'drunk tanks,' hospitals, Communist Party meeting rooms, and outside during the summer. One group in the Elizabeth Church decided we would take the film to the ends of Russia—until we reached Japan or Alaska."

"How far did you get, Mikhail?"

"All the way to the islands next to Alaska, where the Aleuts live," he said proudly. "We enlisted film teams from our church and sent them out for six weeks to three months."

I pulled out a map of the Soviet Union from my briefcase. His finger traced a path across Kazakhstan and the Central Asia republics, past Novosibirsk to the Krasnoyarsk area.

"Here was our first stop," he pointed. "It's the little city of Sharypovo."

I found it on my map. "What happened there?"

"When we got there, there was no church and not one believer. Now twenty people come to a church that meets each week in a house."

Faithful, they continued to push east.

"Our next evangelism was in Ulan Ude, Buryatia," he said.

I remembered hearing an impassioned plea from a lone Buryat believer asking for people to evangelize her area. The Buryats were one of the least-reached groups of people in the world.

"Did you see any Buryats come to Christ?" I inquired.

"Yes. I don't remember all the places, but two 15-year-old girls received Christ when we showed it in a home for children. We also showed it in a maximum security prison where every person there had been convicted of murder. After one showing, a prisoner gave us all the money he had saved and told us, 'I want everyone in Buryatia to see this film.'"

Mikhail continued to open the map wider until we reached the east coast of Russia.

"Did you get this island down here by Japan?" I asked, half in jest.

"Yes, we did," he smiled back. "I didn't go on that trip, but we covered most of the major cities on the Sakhalin Island, starting with Yuzhno Sakhalinsk."

He pointed to another spot on the map. "Then we went on to Kamchatka Peninsula. We were there a whole month," he beamed. Receiving permission from the officials to show the film whenever they wanted, the film team showed it every day. "We had crowds of fifty to eight hundred each night." Mikhail brightened and leaned forward. "At the end of a month, there were so many new believers that one of the men from my church decided to stay for three more months to help the new churches that have been formed there."

I sat amazed. These were not "trained" evangelists. These were just men and women, gripped by the Spirit of God, who kept going to the ends of the earth, whether anyone knew about it or not.

"In between our trips to the east, our people in Elizabeth Church showed the film around our own city of Krasnodar. Near one city is a camp for political prisoners. When they went to show the film, the only appropriate place was the wall where Lenin's picture was hanging. The Communist Party had not yet fallen into disfavor, so it was a brave political move when the commandant took the picture down and growled, 'Show the film.' "

"Today fifteen prisoners attend the church in the prison camp."

"Who is the pastor?" I asked.

"One of the prisoners leads it. They all became believers on the same day, but one of them was willing to be the leader of the group."

"How is the church doing?"

"I talked to the prison officials not too long ago," he answered, "and they said those prisoners who are now believers show a whole new attitude. They do their work without being pressured, which is unusual."

Mikhail turned back to the map. "Here is where we went on our last trip," he said, pointing to Bering Island, eleven time zones east of Moscow. "Not far from the coast of Alaska, it is home to the Aleuts, another of the world's unreached people groups."

"How did you get there? What was it like? How far is it?" I was full of questions.

"About 360 miles off the shore of Kamchatka. We actually got the military to take us there by helicopter and Coast Guard cutter."

I was amazed. The Soviet Navy had helped reach the Aleuts for Christ!

"The people on the island were very glad to see us. There had been no believers on that island for seventy years. They told us we were like angels coming to visit them. More than ten thousand Aleuts saw the film, and many are eager to know much more about Jesus. The governor of the Aleuts region wrote a letter of thank you on behalf of all the people, inviting us to come back."

I couldn't help wondering who gave the funds to buy that projector and copy of the film. What a powerful investment for the kingdom of God. It illustrated again that we were doing the right things in The JESUS Film Project.

Many of us can't learn another language and move to another culture, though there is still a tremendous need for missionaries. But we can equip national believers in various countries with films, follow-up literature, vehicles, and support so they can keep taking the message to those remote corners of the earth.

Perhaps more of us need to be "bridges" or non-residential missionaries. That is, we need to pick an unreached area of the world and determine that we will do all we can to reach it, right from where we live. It may mean traveling there to do some evangelism if it is needed and permitted, then helping to get the films and follow-up materials translated and printed. And, finally, it might mean sending training teams in to equip the new believers for their ministry.

So much has happened. But there's still so much to do. While I rejoiced in the wonderful work of Mikhail and the four churches in his area, I remembered a letter from another pastor who had received his projector at the same time as Mikhail.

He recounted his efforts to take the film into the remote areas of Siberia:

> We arrived at a village of several hundred people who had never had a film shown. They had no electricity, but we found a generator and finally the whole village gathered. We turned the projector on, but it quit. We had been showing the film so much, I'm afraid the projector just died.
>
> We had to leave the village that night without showing the film, and we have not been back. We have no projector. Can you help us?

And so the challenge goes on, to keep taking the film to the world, something we really can do together!

As the march of the "JESUS" film across the former Soviet Union intensified, many new opportunities for involvement opened up. General John Jackson, who had spoken so eloquently at the Georgian theatrical premiere, was now invited to address the Georgian veterans of the war in Afghanistan.

Vietnam. Afghanistan. Two unpopular wars. Other people's wars. For soldiers in the Soviet Union, the parallel between their involvement in Afghanistan and the Americans in Vietnam was striking.

On a gray, rainy morning in Tbilisi, I watched ex-soldiers file into a small meeting room. There were no uniforms, but the horrible results of their involvement in war were apparent. Some were scarred. Some hobbled with canes. Half of the men in the room had been wounded.

The tiny republic of Georgia had sent 4,000 men into battle; 123 never returned. Hundreds of others who did were wounded. Now these veterans had formed a group to support one another. The leader had hosted us at a marvelous feast in his home the night before. He began to speak slowly:

"General Jackson, we welcome you. We have many things in common. When you were flying combat missions in Vietnam, you were being shot at with weapons given to the North Vietnamese by us. And when we were in Afghanistan, we were being shot at with Stinger missiles that you supplied to the Afghan Muhajadeen rebels. I think that it's time for both of our governments to get out of the war business." There were smiling nods of agreement all over the room among both the Americans and the Soviets.

Deeply moved, General Jackson rose to speak. "While I was in Vietnam, I faced three difficult situations and questions: 1) the eternal loneliness; 2) what if I died?; and 3) how could I possibly handle the death of my friends?" He paused for the translator.

"During this difficult time, I found that only God could give me the peace of heart that I needed." He went on to describe how his commitment to Christ had brought him through those days of loneliness and separation. "In Washington, D.C., there is a memorial to those who died in the Vietnam War, a wall with all of their names inscribed into it. I cannot walk along that wall without tears. Among those listed are the names of many of my friends. Friends who took off one morning to fly a mission and never returned. Why did I live? Perhaps it is because God has a plan for me."

The veterans were invited to respond. A dark-haired man, choking with emotion, rose to speak. "General Jackson, when we were in Afghanistan, our Soviet commander would not allow us to speak about trusting in God. If we were caught wearing a cross or a religious medal, we were thrown into military prison."

Then he pulled out a little medallion with a picture of Jesus. "But I did not listen. Through the war I held on to this image of Jesus in my hand." He walked forward slowly and gave the medal to General Jackson.

"Jesus brought me through the war. I want to give this to you as a gift to remember us."

With deep appreciation and just a little reluctance, General Jackson received the precious treasure.

Others rose to ask questions:

"Will you help us set up our veterans association?"

"Can you help us to get back the four Georgians who never returned from war? One is a prisoner in Pakistan."

"Can we set up some exchange visits between our veterans and yours?"

And then it was over. John led the group in a prayer, inviting them to receive Jesus as their personal Savior. He pointed out how Jesus could fill the void and heal the inner hurts.

We had experienced another powerful, spiritual hour in these early days of the opening Soviet Union.

A few days after this moving experience in Georgia, I went back to Moscow to do some filming in Red Square with Bill Bright. With things still under Communist rule, it was unusual to have a foreign film crew in Red Square. We wanted to shoot a short video that would encourage people to provide funds for the films and projectors needed in every part of the country.

Before long, a huge crowd gathered, listening to us. Fund-raising appeals always make me uneasy. I don't ever want to be a part of anything that smacks of manipulation or exaggeration. And I don't like to talk about the people we are trying to reach in their presence.

In any event, Bill suggested that we take a break in the shooting and just talk to some folks, one on one. Up to that point in early 1990, I had never known of anyone witnessing in Red

Square. Now, hundreds of groups have done it, but at that time it was still a little risky.

We passed out a few *Four Spiritual Laws* booklets and soon a group of fifty-plus began clamoring for copies. We had no more, so I began to explain to the group what was in the booklet. My interpreter was a twenty-year-old student who had spent the last two years caring for mice in a research lab—not a particularly outgoing type of person.

But he interpreted for me as best he could. I read through the booklet and then explained that they could receive Christ and become followers of Jesus by simply asking Him to forgive their sins and inviting Him to come into their lives. Nobody in the crowd left. I said I would repeat the prayer slowly, aloud. If they wanted to talk to God, right there on the street, and tell Him they wanted to accept His Son as the payment for their sins, they could follow along as I said the words of the prayer.

At the end of the prayer, I asked how many had repeated it with me to receive Jesus as the payment for their sins. About twenty lifted their hands. One was a young professional man in his forties. His face radiant, he was overcome with emotion. He couldn't get over the fact that he could now talk directly with God. In the middle of this Communist nation, he was saying, "I will go with God."

Through the next several years, the picture of his face in my mind constantly reminded me of the Russian people's hunger to know God. Author Philip Yancy said on his return from Russia about the same time, "Never in all my years have I met a people with such a ravenous appetite for God." I agree.

One year later new opportunities still continued to unfold. The ministry of Campus Crusade for Christ obtained permission to use the Communist Party Hall of Congresses for five Easter concerts. At each concert there would be a brief presentation of the gospel. Dr. Bright asked me to do the first presentation.

The 150-voice choir finished the first half of their concert about 11:30 on the Saturday morning of Easter weekend. I walked to the podium and looked out at the crowd of more than two thousand people.

Simply being in this building was a miracle. Eighteen months earlier, as I had toured the grounds of the Kremlin, our guide told us in no uncertain terms that foreigners were not permitted inside the Hall of Congresses. From time to time, we in the West saw only pictures of Gorbachev speaking in front of this vast auditorium at a Communist Party gathering, or some meeting of the parliament.

But now we were having a Christian evangelistic concert and the approvals for the use of the hall had all been signed by the KGB. I looked at the approval form and thanked the Lord that He had people everywhere who could make things happen in His timing. This was His time and a new friend got the paperwork taken care of for us.

One of my Russian contacts raised his eyebrows a little when I told him how the permit had been secured. "We know your friend," he said. "He has been KGB for years. I'm surprised you want to deal with such people."

However, the auditorium had been secured, and I gave the message. I spoke briefly on man's thirst to find meaning and purpose in life and ultimately to make his own peace with God.

At the end of the message I again gave the audience a chance to pray a prayer of invitation to receive Christ, just about the same as I had done with the group on the corner of Red Square by the GUM department store. And in response, across that auditorium a sea of hands went up, with about 60 percent of the people saying they were receiving Jesus as their personal Savior.

To be sure, we had much more work to do. Some simply indicated they were taking a step toward God. Others were saying they no longer wanted to be atheists. But some understood clearly what they were doing, and they were overjoyed to finally know just how one could come to God.

As far as I know, I was the first person to preach the gospel in that Hall of Congresses in the Kremlin. It was an awesome privilege, but nothing to dwell on. The next day, Dr. Bright would speak on the resurrection not only to the full auditorium, but to an additional fifty million people watching on national television.

What a thrill to repeatedly see so many men and women, adults, coming to the Lord. But what about the children? I began thinking more and more about their special needs.

CHAPTER 20

The Soviet Schools Open

Could we show the film in every school in the Soviet Union? How should we begin? Who would set it up? How could it be paid for? Lots of questions, few answers. In any event, we had no time to think about it now. During the next five months, every available person on our staff would be involved in the theatrical releases of the film. Contracts had been signed with fifteen studios, and we were in a flat-out sprint to get the film translated and checked to meet the schedule of every premiere.

We were showing in theaters in fifteen areas of the Soviet Union and Eastern Europe. Seventeen language translations were under way. Twelve million Gospels of Luke were being printed.

We could do nothing but set aside our concerns for the school children for the time being.

Each week brought the opening of the film in a new country or Soviet republic. And each week was filled with crisis. So much to do in such a short time. Complete the translation of the film in the proper language. Verify the translation. Make the film copies. Ship. Clear customs. Organize the premiere tour. Translate, print, and ship the Gospels of Luke. Air shipments lost. Truck shipments lost. Cargo in customs—held up by KGB conservatives, and on and on.

When the final three cities of our first wave of theaters opened, I breathed a sigh of relief. We had not missed a single opening. With a few minor exceptions, it had been perfect.

A few words in the Slovak translation had to be adjusted. The drawings in the *Four Spiritual Laws* for Lithuania had a mistake or two. A misprint was discovered in the Gospel of Luke for Czecho-slovakia, so the booklets were reprinted. Reports came that a few Gospels of Luke were ending up on the black market; the demand for Scriptures was so great that our shippers and theater managers were stealing them.

By December, the theatrical releases were progressing at a phenomenal rate, and millions were seeing the film. But something else happened that we were not prepared for. It centered around the premiere showings.

As a part of our contracts with the studios in individual countries, we asked them to sponsor a gala premiere, and a party after the performance. A logical thing to do, but totally out of missionary context.

Which is exactly why we did it. We knew if we gave any hint that we were interested in the mission of the film beyond making money, they would be suspicious. So we argued with the studio directors about the dubbing contracts, and how the profits from the theatrical showings would be divided, and into which banks they would be placed, and how the accounting would be verified.

In the United States, for example, one quarter of one percent of all ticket revenue is paid to an independent accounting firm that goes from theater to theater and verifies that the local theater operator is not cheating on the distributor by keeping some of the receipts or reporting fewer people than attended.

No person in the Soviet Union had ever heard of such a thing. The government owned the theaters. The government paid the workers. The government got all the money, all the profits.

However, as things began to open up politically, the theater operators saw an opportunity for a little capitalistic enterprise, and they were interested—especially if the contacts might lead to a future trip to the United States.

God was going before us. The negotiations went well. We decided at the beginning to pay every studio the same amount. The film business is a small world unto itself and the heads of the various studios in Eastern Europe all knew each other and could easily check what we were paying. If we gave in to a higher price for one country, we soon would be asked for more from all the rest.

Our resolve was put to the test in Latvia. A few weeks before the film was to open in Riga, we received a telex stating that the deal was off unless we doubled the amount we were paying.

We sent back a telex saying we were sorry that we would not be able to work together. We could not increase the amount we were offering, but to show our good will, we would purchase a new typewriter for them that they had requested. The next day we received a telex giving the go-ahead for the contract.

However, another stipulation of the contracts proved far more successful than we had ever hoped. We asked that each studio invite the political, cultural, religious, and Communist Party officials in the area to the premiere showing.

We reasoned first that if all the high government officials were seen publicly watching this film about God, it would be difficult for them to crack down on other people watching it. By their presence, they would be giving tacit approval for its showing anywhere. We knew that after the theater showings were completed, Christians would show it in other locations, and we didn't want them to get in trouble or be persecuted for it.

Second, we hoped that we would reach the leadership when they viewed the film, and that perhaps they would open up other opportunities in the future.

And the leaders came. In Bulgaria, the president, vice president, prime minister, and half of the cabinet attended. In Russia, seven out of the nine ministers in the cabinet, and the chief advisors to Boris Yeltsin all turned out.

Invariably, the minister or deputy minister of education of every country and language came to the premiere in their area.

And without exception, every one of them asked our representatives if we would show the "JESUS" film in their school system to their students.

It began in Tbilisi, Georgia. God had begun to move in answer to our prayers for the children!

In the flickering blue-white light given off by the film projector, I studied the faces of the children watching "JESUS." They sat mesmerized, totally captivated by the story. And more. Because this was not just any movie. This was not just another story. This was about God. These were the words of Jesus. The film was about how to live forever.

And then I remembered where we were. In the Soviet Union! In schools controlled by the Communist Party! Now, just six months after the first public showings in theaters, we were having the first showing in a Soviet public school!

I was back in Tbilisi on a Saturday, when schools were closed. Yet, when I made it known that we could have a special showing for a school, they opened the doors wide. The teachers and students welcomed us with much ceremony.

As we entered the large foyer of the school, students and teachers, dressed for a very special occasion, met us. One by one, ten-year-old girls with freshly braided hair and colorful ribbons came forward carrying bouquets of flowers for us. Smiles shy and cheeks blushing, they welcomed us with well-practiced English greetings. "Good afternoon, honored guests from America. We are happy to welcome you to our school." A slight curtsy and it was the next one's turn.

Each of the best speakers in their English classes delivered a short greeting. Then in our honor, they quoted for us Edgar Allen Poe's "The Raven."

We toured their school, talked with the teacher, and moved to one of the larger classrooms to show the film.

At the scenes of the crucifixion, some covered their eyes. Others shed silent tears. This was the story of the Son of the God of the universe who came to die for their sins. This was personal, and oh, so meaningful.

When the invitation to receive Christ was given by the narrator at the end of the film, all the students and teachers began to pray the prayer out loud, with no embarrassment. Who wouldn't want to receive Christ?

Afterwards, I presented a copy of the film and the 16mm projector to the Georgia school system to be used in different schools each week. I was elated! What an incredible break-through!

While I was rejoicing in Soviet Georgia, Dr. Bright was in a Ukrainian school, a thousand miles away, with a similar showing. As I watched the film report a few days later, I was struck again with the incredible hunger of the Soviet people to know God.

The showing of the film in this Ukrainian school was a land-mark event. Six hundred students and teachers crowded the auditorium. Again, rapt attention. Excitement at the miracles. Audible gasps at the crucifixion. Tears at the burial. Radiant smiles at the resurrection.

And then Dr. Bright spoke. "The greatest day of my life was the day I received Christ as my own personal Savior."

He asked how many had prayed the prayer of invitation to receive Christ, and more than half raised their hands in response.

The Young Pioneers, wearing their traditional red bandannas, passed out a copy of the *Four Spiritual Laws* to each student. This was the first organization in the Communist youth system for children from eight to fifteen years old. From the Young Pioneers they advance to Comsomol, the Young Communist League. After Comsomol, a few would get invitations to join the Communist Party.

Yet, incredibly, here in this Soviet high school, the Young Pioneers were distributing the *Four Spiritual Laws*. Bill explained the content of the booklet briefly and showed them the prayer in the back that they could pray if they had not yet placed their faith in Jesus.

It was an awesome day. The teachers were then asked to come forward if they would like to receive a Bible. With shy smiles, wiping the wrinkles from their dresses, they stepped forward. What an incredible gift. Worth a month's salary, and impossible to obtain, it was now a free gift to them.

And in America? None of what was taking place here could happen in America. At that moment, Soviet schools had more freedom to preach the gospel than did our own schools.

Six months after our first school showing in Tbilisi, the highest school officials in fifteen countries had asked us to come and show the film.

But by December 17, 1990, we were nearing the point of total exhaustion. So much had been happening for the cause of the kingdom. Three days before that, we had finished the fourteenth and fifteenth premieres—in Budapest, Hungary, and in Bucharest, Romania. More invitations to show the film in the schools had been offered, but someone else would have to do it. We were just too spent. At a Christmas celebration with our staff, I realized that everyone was as exhausted as I was. It was a good kind of tired, though. We had given ourselves for the cause of the kingdom.

I gave them a few words of thanks before they left for the holidays to be with their families and friends and to rest. "I will never be able to repay you for the sacrifices you have made during these last months, but because of you and those who have provided the funds, many thousands of people in the former Soviet Union will celebrate their first real Christmas this year as members of God's family."

Through the next several weeks, as strength gradually returned, I began to think about the children again. What if every school child in Russia could see the film? If it now would be possible for them to hear the gospel, how better to ensure that their first impression of Jesus be the true and accurate account contained in the "JESUS" film?

One evening after watching the film footage from our first school showings, I decided that reaching the schools in the USSR was something we had to at least attempt. The Lord had never let the thoughts leave my mind. He had given me a burden and a vision I could not put aside.

So we plunged in with great enthusiasm.

Estonia was the most open. Spencer Brand, a veteran Campus Crusade staff leader from Washington, would go to Tallin, Estonia, in February to see the Ministry of Education. They had seemed the most insistent that we should do something immediately.

Then I realized that, on my way to Mongolia to get the same kind of distribution agreement we had with Russia, I would have a one-day stop in Moscow. I thought, *Perhaps I can get an appointment with the Department of Education during the layover.*

We telexed our contacts in Moscow who had helped with the theatrical release and got an appointment with the deputy minister.

However, the war with Iraq broke out, one day before I was scheduled to leave the U.S. In the early hours, America glued itself to the TV. CNN reported live from Baghdad as the bombs dropped. Iraq launched Scud missiles against Israel and Saudi Arabia.

The U.S. State Department discouraged travel. Airports doubled their security, and then doubled it again. According to reports, Iraq was sending terrorists to every major airport. Travelers were urged to stay away from London Heathrow and Frankfurt airports. My schedule would take me by Pan Am right through Frankfurt. Everyone canceled travel plans. Two businessmen, Mike Hockett and Jim Blankemeyer, called me to see if the trip was still on.

Emotionally, I wanted to cancel it. What difference would it make to the Mongolian studio officials if we came a month or two later? My family wanted me to stay. The hour-by-hour news reports from the front were frightening and the children were nervous. This television war was all too real. What should I do? What was the right decision to be made as a husband and a father?

I prayed. I wanted to delay the trip. What if I took these men to the USSR and something happened? Would I be risking their lives? Their wives and families were uneasy as well. They'd have to make their own decisions. I prayed again. "Lord, for seventy years, Your people have been trying to get into Mongolia with the gospel. Now the appointment is set with the government film studios. Will something happen if we change dates? Also, the appointment in Moscow with the deputy of education is set. What do I do?" I asked.

I heard no audible voice, but I felt a strong, undeniable impression that I should go as planned. I felt a confident assurance and peace that the decision was right. My friends who were accompanying me felt the same way.

But what would I say to the minister of education? How many schools were there? How many students?

I called a congressman friend and asked if he could get answers to those questions from our intelligence department. His aide called back a few hours later with, "There are 135,000 schools in the Soviet Union with 42 million students; 65,000 of the schools are in Russia."

We could not put together enough film teams to get to 135,000 schools. We would have to get the school officials themselves to show it to the students.

I tried my idea out on several of The JESUS Film Project leaders to get a reality check. They said, "If you give a video to all those schools, you know they'll show it. And if they show it, lots of children are going to receive Christ. And when they do, who will follow them up?"

"I don't know," I shrugged. "Maybe we could get one teacher from each school to come to a three-day convocation. If they receive Christ, maybe we could teach them how to follow up the children. In fact, maybe we could develop a course on Christian ethics and morality that could include some of the follow-up materials. I don't know what the response would be, but we could try."

On January 23 we arrived in Moscow, and at ten the next morning we entered the office of Eugene Kurkin, deputy minister of education for the Russian Republic. We sat around a conference table under a large framed picture of Lenin and began the meeting.

I told the deputy minister about the good reception we'd had at the theatrical premieres and explained my vision for the course on Christian ethics and morality as a foundation for society.

He leaned back in his chair, folded his hands, and spoke pensively. "We don't know how many caverns there are in the foundation of our society after seventy years without God. You are making a very generous offer to give a film for every school. Do you know how many schools there are in the Russian Republic?"

"I think so," I replied.

He answered, "65,000," as though he was sure I couldn't know that.

"Are you prepared to give a copy of the 'JESUS' video to all those schools?" he continued, a little incredulous at the thought.

I quickly multiplied the 65,000 times the $20 cost per video and realized it could be as much as $1.3 million and then said, "Yes, we are." I didn't know where we would get the money, but this was not the time to think of that. This was the time to open the door for the gospel.

We talked about various aspects of the plan. If they approved it, how many American teachers would come to Russia to help introduce the course? Who would pay for what?

Then he said, "It's interesting that you should come on this day. We have 89 school districts in the Republic of Russia. We will have two or three representatives from each one in Moscow tomorrow for a special meeting of the Ministry of Education. We are going to discuss the whole issue of the separation of church and state. We will present your proposal and then let you know."

I knew then why I had been impressed to go in spite of the start of the war. God has perfect timing. A delayed trip would have missed this annual meeting of their leaders. God is sovereign!

"Would you like to see the 'JESUS' film at your meeting?" volunteered Juli Gusman, our Moscow distributor who had arranged our session. "We will bring a 35mm copy over from Dom Kino."

The deputy minister thought it would be great.

"We will also bring Gospels of Luke for everyone," Juli added. "These will be copies of the script."

The meeting concluded with warm handshakes and some discussion of what we might do in 278 teacher colleges. And the promise to consider a pilot project for leaders from a thousand schools.

As we walked from the meeting, our hearts rejoiced. Later that day, one of the men asked how much the test project would cost.

"About $100,000," I estimated.

"Let me know how much you need. I don't think I can do it all, but don't let finances stop the test," he said.

Incredible! I thought. What a joy to see the body of Christ pull together for the cause of the kingdom. That cooperation on the project was only the beginning.

Five days later I called Moscow from Hong Kong. "Did you see the film?" I asked the minister's interpreter.

"Yes, we did. And we all got copies of the booklet about Jesus. All four hundred of us."

"Did you make a decision about the school project?"

"Yes, we want to go ahead."

We were off! We set out to do the seemingly impossible. How would we write, translate, print, and ship all the materials needed in less than a hundred days? But we laid out a plan, and we went to work.

Through the next several weeks, the willingness of people to help with the project was like nothing I have ever seen. I called Blair Cook, a long-term veteran of the Campus Crusade ministry overseas who was between assignments.

"I want to tell you about an idea I have."

At a convocation held in Vologda, Russia, Dr. Blair Cook (right) presents Paul Eshleman with a copy of the Christian Morals and Ethics curriculum.

"Tell me what you're thinking," he smiled. "I'm always interested in a good challenge."

"People in the Soviet Union write on their response cards at the theaters that they no longer have any basis for belief. They don't respect the government or the Communist Party. They say they no longer know what is right and what is wrong."

I paused for a breath, and then continued. "I have approached the Ministry of Education in Russia to see if they would be willing to bring one principal or one teacher from each school together for a three- or four-day convocation. We would give each teacher a video copy of the 'JESUS' film for their school and show them how to teach a course called 'Christian Ethics and Morality: A Foundation for Society.' We have a chance to impact the whole Soviet Union school system.

"So here is my idea: How would you feel about heading the process of putting the course together and conducting the first test, if we can get a number of educators to agree?"

"It sounds fantastic," Blair responded. "Why don't you let my wife and me pray about it? I'll call you in a day or so."

He called me back the next day with, "We're on! How do we start?"

We finished the phone call with a few clarifications. I would handle the overall strategy, get the first convocation set up, and raise the funds. Blair would develop the curriculum, recruit the instructors, and administer the convocations.

I soon realized that someone would have to live in Moscow to take care of the details of these conferences. But I knew of no one available. So I prayed fervently that the Lord would raise someone up to meet this essential need.

A few days later, Jerry Franks, a businessman and one of our personal supporters, called me.

He and his wife, Karen, came to California from time to time to oversee a hotel they were building. On their last trip, he had mentioned some major financial problems.

I was glad to hear from him now. "How is everything going?" I asked.

"Not that well," he sighed. "In fact, Karen and I have decided to make a change. We'll be in California next week on business. Can we have dinner?"

A week later, my wife, Kathy, and I met them in a lovely restaurant overlooking the ocean. I told him about our remarkable invitation from Moscow. Jerry was interested, but not ready to jump into anything immediately. It was March 16, 1990, only eight weeks until the first conference was scheduled to open in Moscow.

After dinner we drove by to look at our offices. When we finished the tour, I showed them the five-minute report on the showings of the "JESUS" film in Russia. As the pictures of the Soviet children came on the screen, the God who orchestrates the universe touched their hearts.

"What kind of help do you need?" Jerry asked.

"We need someone to move to Moscow and set up all the convocations for the next year," I answered. "Right now we don't have anyone to send. If we don't find someone, we may not be able to hold these conferences."

"Karen and I will pray about it, and we'll let you know Monday."

"Wouldn't it be great if the Lord sent them to work with us?" Kathy commented on the drive home. "They are perfect for the job."

I agreed. Jerry had the educational background; he had once been the superintendent of a Christian school.

On Monday, Jerry called and said, "We're ready to go. This is not what we had planned, but we feel God wants us to do it for at least the next year. What's the next step?"

"Get your passport," I said. "We need to go to Moscow."

On April 2, we left for Moscow. On April 3, we rented Jerry and Karen an apartment. On April 4, we met with the Ministry of Education to begin work on contractual arrangements. And on May 15, Jerry and Karen moved into their apartment in Moscow— eight weeks after our dinner in California.

The meeting at the Ministry of Education was extremely difficult. New people had been assigned to work on the project. Some had not the slightest bit of spiritual interest. Others were hard-core Communists. Gorbachev was still in power; the party had not yet collapsed. There was much opposition internally, but we pressed on.

Meanwhile, back in our offices, preparations went "full-speed ahead." People asked how various parts of the plan would work. I had no idea. We had to assume that we could do everything we planned until someone stopped us or gave a better suggestion.

Early in January 1991, the plan had begun to take shape. I wrote down all of my ideas and began to recruit help. The "to-do" list seemed endless when we began to divide up the responsibilities.

Curt and Lois Mackey and the International Training Office for Campus Crusade for Christ would oversee the development of the curriculum. Research would be done all over the U.S. to see what was presently being taught on Christian ethics and what material was already available. Stan Oakes, heading up the Christian Leadership ministry among college professors, would help recruit potential instructors. Blair would pull together a task force to develop the curriculum, and he would talk personally with Os Guiness, R. C. Sproul, Bruce Wilkinson, Rex Johnson, and a host of other potential advisors.

Sheryl Rose would help coordinate the translation and the ordering of materials. Vernie Schorr would develop the curriculum and material for primary school students. Eric Brogan would help with the printing and shipping of tons of needed materials. Fred West would assist with the fund raising.

Josh McDowell offered to give each teacher a copy of three of his books: *More Than a Carpenter, Evidence That Demands a Verdict,* and *The Resurrection Factor.* All had been translated into Russian. The International Bible Society provided a New Testament for each teacher. A foundation made Gospels of Luke available to every teacher in every one of the 65,000 schools. University professors took time off from their busy teaching schedules to write curriculum, edit materials, and volunteer as instructors.

On May 14, we arrived in Moscow for the first convocation, slated to begin the next day.

But everything was in chaos.

CHAPTER 21

Russian Teachers Welcome the Gospel

May 15 dawned with a bright sun and warm weather. After the long, cold winter in Moscow, spirits were lighter, trees boasted leaves, and the last of the ugly brown slush along the streets had melted. Two hundred and fifty teachers and principals would be attending this first convocation for teachers. It was a historic event, a day for praising the Lord.

But we were in deep trouble.

Two truckloads of materials had been impounded by customs authorities. We had shipped them in from Germany, and the authorities would not release them until the proper paperwork had been completed. Some inside sources told us that conservative religious officials, informed by border guards of the incoming materials, had gone to Yeltsin's office and obtained an order to confiscate them. It was not especially surprising, just one more hurdle to overcome. That was how things worked under the Communists.

We had no Bibles, no New Testaments, no Gospels of Luke or follow-up materials. No curriculum, no notebooks, no student notes, and none of the gifts we had brought for the teachers.

We did have the "JESUS" videos, some books by Josh McDowell, and a few materials we had brought with us on the plane. Those would have to do. We would begin anyway.

During the next three days, I worked eighteen to twenty hours a day trying to get the materials released, or to secure replacements. We immediately sent telexes to the U.S. to reprint all materials and air-ship them to Russia as soon as possible. We had conferences scheduled in two more cities, and we needed the materials for them, even if we missed receiving the materials in Moscow.

I worked at creating new documents and getting them signed by different officials. Hour after hour I sat in the Cosmos Hotel business center, cutting and pasting, getting new forms translated into Russian, and hoping they now said the right things. We desperately needed high-ranking members of the Ministry of Education to sign for the importation of the materials. Many were afraid to take this step, and even after the papers were signed, other officials still blocked us.

On the first day, Jerry Franks and I spent ten hours driving from one warehouse to the next to pick up some Bibles we had secured from other groups working in the city. The Moscow Project, sponsored by the International Bible Society and others, provided the New Testaments needed. We also went to the theater distributors and gathered up Gospels of Luke for the teachers.

On the third day, the truck drivers informed us that if we didn't clear up the paperwork in the next twelve hours, they were heading back to Germany. Ten hours later we had made only slight progress. I sent runners out on the streets in the neighborhood where the trucks had last been spotted to offer the drivers another hundred dollars each day if they would stay until the problem was resolved. They agreed to wait at least one more day.

Meanwhile, the convocation was about to get underway. With or without materials, we had to begin.

We were breaking new ground. No one had ever before tried to do what we were doing. We could not stop now.

Our first convocation in Moscow was to be held in the suburb of Perova in a Pioneer Palace, the home of the Communist Youth Movement. The Communist Party had built these "palaces" in every community. They housed all the extracurricular activity of school children from ages eight to fifteen.

They looked a great deal like a well-equipped YMCA in our own country. The buildings contained a gymnasium, classrooms, and an auditorium. The children would come every day after school for classes in music, dance, art, crafts, gymnastics, drama, and much more. When I met with the Ministry of Education officials, I learned that there were thousands of these palaces and hundreds of summer camps.

As we entered that Pioneer Palace on the first morning, we were greeted by a big, and very imposing, Communist educational official. He was not smiling.

"Welcome to Moscow," he said, knitting his forehead into a frown. "I am Gernady Fyodorov. We want to welcome you here, but I want to give you a word of warning. If these sessions are boring, no one will come back this afternoon."

His intimidating welcome had not come as a surprise. We had been told several times that Russian teachers would walk out if they were bored. We brought the best instructors we could, but had decided we also would give some book or piece of material away every six hours or so during the conference. Now, with so many of the materials in customs, we were concerned.

We need not have worried. The materials we had vanished quickly, and attendance increased every day.

The content of the conference teaching was built around four major themes.

The first introduced the listeners to the Christian worldview, as contrasted to a Marxist worldview. Dr. Udo Middelmann, Dr. Ronald Nash, and other Christian apologists provided a solid intellectual atmosphere. Their strategic overview reached teachers who had no idea what kind of God we were talking about, much less one they could know personally.

The second major theme each morning was on the foundational truths of Christianity. If the teachers were to understand the ethical and moral foundations that come from Christianity, they needed to know the basic tenets of the faith. During these sessions, we showed the "JESUS" film—because almost everything we know about God, we have learned through Jesus. After the showing was over, we gave them their own opportunity to receive Jesus as their personal Savior if they had never done so.

The third emphasis was on helping them become better teachers. We taught them how to use story-telling, role-playing, and other interactive learning methods, quite a contrast for teachers who had always used the lecture method. But they were extremely interested in how teaching is done in the West. During this time, the teachers actually practiced teaching certain stories from the Bible using these methods. It was thrilling to watch teachers, who

Small groups of Russian public school teachers gather to discuss how to teach the Christian Ethics and Morality curriculum in their classrooms.

had never held a Bible before, go into a small group and prepare a lesson on the prodigal son.

The final part of the convocation involved dividing the teachers into groups of eight to ten people. Each small group had its own interpreter to assist with the communication. Small group leaders who came primarily from North America helped answer questions and make the conference personal for each one who attended.

"You should teach your courses and show the 'JESUS' film in all the Pioneer Palaces and the summer camps," the officials had suggested. There were more than 300,000 teachers who could use the Ethics and Morality course.

During the final session, we invited the Russian teachers to share what they had received from the convocation. The responses were extremely moving.

One teacher stood to say that as a fourth-grade teacher she would ordinarily teach the subject of atheism. "We know now," she continued seriously, "that atheism is not the way for our country. But we have no money to print new textbooks. Thank you for bringing this new material. I will begin teaching my students about God."

Another teacher stood. "For the last year and a half, I have been trying to teach ethics to my class using fairy tales," she said. "Now I can teach them the truths of God's Word."

Despite all the problems, the conference had been a great success. During every break, educators who had heard we were in the city surrounded us. One university instructor asked if we could help them rewrite all of their textbooks.

"We don't know which parts of our history books are true and which are not," he explained. "Will you help us rewrite them so that they tell the truth? Could you help us take out the Marxist orientation and replace it with a Christian focus? After all, we do have a Christian heritage."

During coffee breaks, officials who wanted to sell us Pioneer Palaces and camps approached us. Others had ideas for us to go on nationwide educational television. It was an open door for the gospel beyond any I have ever seen in my life.

The teachers themselves were overcome with gratefulness as they received the materials we distributed.

I walked into the office of one of the administrators at the Pioneer Palace and caught her wrapping another two Bibles in some newspaper and hiding them behind a plant. We had forgotten one of the rules of Communism: No worker was to have anything that the leaders did not have. We learned that we would have to bring at least a hundred extra sets of materials to each conference just to give away to the officials, on every level, who were involved.

The hunger for materials and learning was insatiable. As the convocations multiplied, we kept learning, too. In many conferences, only half the material could be presented because the speaker had to wait for the interpreter to finish repeating the same phrase in the new language. So in order to have more teaching time, we brought earphones for each teacher and set up simultaneous translation booths.

We decided to hire the professor who trained top simultaneous translators for all political negotiations. Dr. Eugene Breus and his wife, Zlata, had translated for years for the Soviet delegation at the United Nations. They were very, very good.

Simultaneous translation is essential to every convocation.

Still, at this first convocation, we believed we had to have our own Russian speaker from the United States to listen to the interpreters and make sure they were not changing the message as they were translating it. Eugene brought with him the men and women who had been doing the interpreting for the trade negotiations with the U.S. and some of the commentators from Radio Moscow. We didn't do everything perfectly in the conference, but the Russian educators appreciated the attention we gave to ensure the accuracy of the written materials and the professionalism of the interpreters.

Newspaper reporters began to crowd the hallways after the sessions. They were amazed at how the conference was run. They had never seen time cards before to tell the speakers that it was time for them to stop their session. All of their articles spoke of the "highly organized Americans."

But the real impact of that first convocation was felt and seen in the small groups. The teachers had come in the first day wary and cynical. Some had been ordered by their principals to attend. For others, the conference had been a "payoff" for some favor rendered in the past.

In the small group meetings on the first day, many teachers announced that they were members of the Communist Party; they were atheists; they would not become believers; they had come because they were interested in the teaching methods of the West. Many sat with arms folded—some were big, imposing, intimidating Russian women with scowls of cynicism, hardened by years of hate, mistrust, and lies.

On the second day, we showed the "JESUS" film, and I spoke for thirty minutes after the showing to explain how one begins a personal relationship with God.

"It doesn't do any good to teach people to follow a system of morals and ethics if there is no motivation to follow that system," I said. "People need to do the right thing, even when no one is looking. We believe that if people make a commitment to the God of the universe, to follow His ways, they will do the right thing because they are motivated from within. This faith in God also will give them the supernatural strength to do the right thing even when it is difficult.

A Russian school teacher receives a videocassette copy of "JESUS" that she will take back to her students.

"If we are going to place this kind of faith in God, we need to know what He is like. That's why we have shown you this film on the life of Jesus. He said that He came to show us what God is like. He is like Jesus.

"Today, if you would like to become a follower of Jesus, if you would like to accept the payment that Jesus made for your sins so that you can live forever with the God who made the universe, I am going to help you talk to Him in prayer.

"I realize that for some of you, this may be your first prayer ever. Others of you were taught some of these things by your grandmother many years ago, but you pushed them aside. Perhaps you still have many questions but you want to take your first steps toward God. I want to help you today to say a simple prayer to Him."

I then led them in a prayer of invitation to Jesus. It was a chance for them to receive Him as Savior and Lord. They needed so much more follow-up, but this was a beginning.

By the end of the fourth day, we knew that we would need even more time to get the materials out of customs. We announced to the teachers that they would have to return in a few weeks to pick up the rest of their materials. They were skeptical. The government often promised them things and never delivered. There was never enough to go around. It was a fact of life.

However, they had received a Bible, some New Testaments, Gospels of Luke, a couple of Christian books, and the "JESUS" video, so they were grateful. They would be unable to begin teaching the curriculum, however, until they could get the instruction manual.

We got part of the materials a week later and another part about two weeks after that. However, one entire truckload was forever lost somewhere in a "black hole."

But the convocation proceeded wonderfully. Most of our guesses about how the schedule should go and what content should be presented had been right. God had answered our prayers for wisdom and guidance, and, as usual, we were surprised.

What we were only beginning to understand, but a fact that would be emblazoned on our minds and hearts during the next three years, was that this was God's idea. He would keep the doors open, and He would prompt the people to come. Also, He would encourage that one person on the educational committee to stand against all the Communist sympathizers, and He would carry this project forward.

By the end of the conference, 48 percent of those who attended had indicated that they had placed their faith in Christ.

Despite every difficulty, an amazing ministry had been launched. The next generation of Russian children would learn of God in their classrooms, and the first impression many would have of Jesus would come as they viewed the "JESUS" film. We gave thanks and left for the train station. Our agreement was to try the convocations in three cities as a test. Vologda and Leningrad were waiting.

An all-night train ride took us out to the countryside. It was only May, but already the nights were short. I crawled out of my berth at 3:30 a.m. looking for the "water closet" (restroom) as the Russian countryside raced by. Thickets of white birch trees were just coming into bloom, and I saw flowering fields, pine forests, and marshy swamplands.

Spring! A break from the long, bitter winter. Little patches of land developing into gardens. Peasants struggling to raise some vegetables. Everyone trying to survive great food shortages and the continuing economic collapse. I marveled at the goodness of God. What an unspeakable privilege to be going into the heartland of Russia. As spring was breaking the cruel bonds of winter, perhaps God would use us to bring a springtime of faith and break the bonds of cold and barren lives. It was a time of awesome respect and worship, of unspoken thoughts, of high expectancy. We felt deeply thankful that the mighty, loving hand of God reached out to such spiritually starved people.

Vologda was a marked contrast to Moscow. Many houses were built as log cabins. There had once been more than fifty churches here. Now there were two. A third was opening. Still not many for a city of more than 300,000.

The minister of education for the Vologda region met us at the train. This region encompassed 26 districts, 837 schools, and more than 500,000 students. Of the 26 districts, 23 would be represented, and 350 schools would take part. Some leaders had come hundreds of miles and were staying in hotels, and the 50 English teachers from a teacher-training college would eat in factory lunchrooms.

We stayed at the Communist Party hotel. A bust of Lenin sat in the lobby. A Party headquarters and meeting place for the whole region turned into the site for our convocation. In the same auditorium where teachers had been indoctrinated in how to teach atheism, we would teach the truths of God's Word.

But this was the countryside. People here were not as progressive and "liberal" as the folks in Moscow. Most of my life I'd leaned toward the conservative side of things in America. But in the Soviet Union at this time, the liberals were the ones who thought about giving more freedom to Christianity. The conservatives were the old-guard Communist Party officials. I was glad to be a liberal here.

We were excited. Having learned a great deal in the Moscow conference, the small group leaders were much more confident. More than four hundred teachers packed the sessions.

In the opening meeting, the head of the education committee for the region, a high Party official in the area, came down to give the opening speech. We could tell that the teachers had misgivings about even being in the audience. They wondered if they would one day be called to account for their attendance at a meeting about Christian morals and ethics.

The official began his speech by saying, "Of course, all of us here are Communists and atheists. However, under *glasnost*, we are now allowing new ideas to be presented. So we welcome our friends from America and this conference of educational ideas."

Halfway through the conference, some of our materials were released from customs and brought up to Vologda by train.

We had worked hard on the content of our conference to make it high caliber educationally. No Russian educator would have to be embarrassed by sponsoring our conference. They might not like the spiritual content, but they had to be impressed by the philosophical and educational methods taught. The expertise and credentials of the visiting university professors validated the material to even the most ardent skeptics.

We had a fine line to walk. These had to be educational conferences or they would not be co-sponsored by the Ministry of Education. We had to prepare the small group leaders to be especially sensitive in how to bring teachers to the point of commitment within this educational context. Several times in the conference, such as after the "JESUS" film showing, it would be especially appropriate, and we wanted to take advantage of these.

We wanted to move carefully, but there was much spiritual hunger.

On the morning of the second day, my interpreter came to ask a question. "The members of our small group would like to know: How can we open the door to our lives and get Christ, in the way we heard one of the Americans talking about?"

"That's a good question," I smiled. "I will tell you how each of you can personally invite Jesus to enter your life, right after we see the film this morning."

"Okay," she nodded. "We will be waiting."

Later that afternoon, as our small group of teachers met together, we learned that more than half of them had prayed to receive Christ, including my interpreter, the twenty-year-old daughter of the deputy minister of education for the whole region.

As in Moscow, the final session brought many wonderful reports, with many tears, of how the lives of the teachers had been affected in just four days. We were doing important work, and we knew we needed to expand.

When the third convocation closed in Leningrad, the Ministry of Education officials were besieged by requests to invite us to other regions of the country. The showings of the "JESUS" film in the Russian public schools were off and running.

CHAPTER 22

The CoMission

By the end of June 1991, all of our dreams and hopes had been surpassed. I was excited. We actually had completed negotiations with the Ministry of Education officials in Moscow; set up a test to train a thousand teachers; developed, translated, and printed an entire curriculum in Russian; and conducted four conferences. And the response was tremendous. They wanted us to do more conferences. It was intoxicating!

But some of those who had been there with us were not sure we should move so fast. Jerry Franks, Vernie Schorr, and others gave us a very clear message: "We don't want to keep moving on to new cities when these teachers are so eager to grow in the faith. We can't just go off and leave hundreds of teachers without any guidance or encouragement in these cities. It's like giving birth to a new baby and leaving it on a doorstep somewhere. We want to go back to the cities and follow up on them."

I didn't know what to do. They were right, of course. We couldn't just leave these new believers without any help. They had a thousand questions about the Bible, Christianity, and how they could teach the course to their students. What should we do?

We decided to send a follow-up team back once a month to each city. We would also send the teachers a letter each month to stay in touch with them. Jerry organized all of this out of his apartment in Moscow, but we knew it wouldn't be enough. We really needed full-time people in each city.

I pulled out my yellow pad of paper, prayed, and began to write. We would have to move teams of people into each of the cities where we had convocations. There would have to be at least four people on a team—$150 \times 4 = 600$. We would need 600 people to move to Russia for at least a year to begin the discipleship process.

So that was my plan, at least to start with. I didn't announce it to anyone. There were too many unanswered questions. Where would we possibly find six hundred workers willing to move where there was bad housing, food shortages, and the political conditions of the Soviet Union?

I didn't know the answer.

In the past, Dr. Bright had always counseled me: "You make the plan. It's up to God to supply the resources. If the plan needs to be changed, He'll show you along the way. Just as it's easier to steer a moving car, God can guide you more specifically as you move out in faith."

Bill and I had not talked in detail about this particular plan. He had been greatly excited about the newly opened doors in Russia and the other republics. He had been praying for those countries for more than forty years, and now he was enthusiastic about any plans to bring the gospel to them. So I had this plan —but no people.

As I walked across the campus of Colorado State University at our staff conference, Brian Birdsall, the Campus Crusade for Christ director from Dartmouth, flagged me down. "I'm really interested in what you are doing in the Soviet Union," he enthused.

"Well, why don't you tell your supervisor you'd like to make a change and move your family to Moscow? We need you to help follow up all of these thousands of teachers who want to be discipled."

"How would it work?" he asked.

"Check with your supervisor and get his permission to explore further, then come out and talk with us in California when we get back next week," I responded. Brian came out. We talked. And a few months later he and his wife, Cathy, were living in Moscow and beginning the follow-up of the teachers.

The next six weeks were a blur of activity. New convocations were scheduled for the fall. Sufficient money had not been raised, and we were committed not to spend what we didn't have. More materials needed to be translated, and we needed help for Jerry the set-up work. Not enough people were available to train the teachers. We had very few administrative personnel in our own office, and only Brian and his wife were free to do the follow-up for a thousand teachers in four cities.

September 4, 1991, found me in Budapest, Hungary, at a meeting for Christian leaders from the former Soviet Union and Eastern Europe. The agenda centered around what agencies from the West should do to best help their brothers in these newly opening countries. I met with Michael Little of the Christian Broadcasting Network (CBN). As a result of their televising a number of programs, they were receiving millions of inquiries. But few local bodies of believers existed into which to guide these new converts. In a back room of the Hungarian Bible Institute, we huddled together one night with Blair Carlson. He had stopped off on his way to Moscow to set up the Billy Graham year-long campaign in the Commonwealth of Independent States (CIS), as it was being called at that time. Both Blair and Michael were planning even bigger evangelism endeavors, but together we recognized the great need for more local groups of believers to be formed.

I shared an idea. Suppose in each of the public schools we started a video Bible class, to be facilitated by a teacher we had led to Christ. They wouldn't be prepared to teach the Bible yet, but they could serve as leaders of the group if they had the right materials and video follow-up lessons.

Both excited about the prospects, Blair and Michael said, "If you set up the groups, we'll promote them as local opportunities for all of those who want to know more." CBN offered to inform the people on their mailing list where the local groups were meeting.

It was a great time of dreaming together for the cause of the kingdom.

Thursday, September 19, 1991, I was back in the office. A church in Alabama had said they wanted to form the first team of four to go over on the new plan. They wanted to take a city. I was encouraged, but we didn't have any information to give ther about what to do, how they would be trained, or how much would cost. Everything was still in the idea stage. Then I bega realize that we had no videos for the video Bible class. We work lay ahead. How would we recruit the people? Who make up the curriculum for the class? Who would we ge up the school convocation program in our office? How would it all be financed?

About 4 p.m. I received an unexpected call from Bruce Wilkinson, then president of Walk Thru the Bible.

A few years earlier, I had taken Bruce to northern Thailand to see the ministry of the "JESUS" film first-hand. Hugh Maclellan, Pat McMillan, and Gene Rubingh of the International Bible Society went along. We had an amazing time seeing the "JESUS" film being shown, watching people respond, and visiting the follow-up groups of new believers.

On one particular morning we visited a New Life Training Center. The training in these centers consists of about 150 hours of instruction. Trainees are taught how to lead people to Christ, follow up on them, start and lead a small group of their own converts, and teach those converts in turn how to reach out to their own families and villages.

I asked Bruce to lead one of his teaching sessions of Walk Thru the Bible for the trainees at the center. The training was held in a little storefront building. The male trainees slept on the classroom floor at night, and the women slept upstairs. The conditions were bleak, but the faces of the trainees were radiant with the joy of the Lord. After Bruce finished his session, he asked one of the group members to tell who had led him to Christ. He pointed to someone else in the room. When he was asked who led him to Christ, he pointed to a girl in the room. This continued until nine generations of new believers stood in front of us—an incredible thing to witness. Boonma Panthasri, the Thailand director for Campus Crusade for Christ hosting us, told us that he could point to nearly a hundred generations in his own discipleship chain.

Bruce and I tried to grasp what we were seeing. These young Thai Christians not only led their friends and family to Christ, but also helped them to introduce others to Him, who would in turn bring others, and on and on. These believers had spiritual children, spiritual grandchildren, spiritual great-grandchildren, and great-great-great-great-grandchildren—more than we could count.

After that day we went back to the house where we were It was a typical Thai home built on poles about fifteen feet round, in a small village set amid the endless rice paddies of Southeast Asia. Underneath the house, the water buffalo were stabled. Bruce and I needed a little rest so we lay down side by side on grass mats on the highly polished wood floor. It was clean, but very little air moved to give relief from the sultry afternoon heat.

As we rested on the mats, I told Bruce about the thousands of groups of new believers forming, not only here, but also in Nepal, Indonesia, and other places. Campus Crusade provided the leaders of these groups with 150 hours of training.

"Bruce," I said, "if these groups are to become local churches with trained pastors, we must give them much more training and equipping. That's what you do so well. Will you come and help us design the curriculum to help these people develop? We could start with one course, get it translated, and begin testing it in a couple of months."

I was excited! Bruce could meet a critical need for preparation of discipleship materials. He was far better equipped than we were to launch something like this. I waited for his response.

"Well," he hesitated, "we're really already pretty busy. We're printing devotional magazines for eighteen different organizations, and we just don't really have time to do much overseas."

I let it drop. About six months later, I called him again and brought up the subject. Same response. So I didn't call him any more.

Now he was calling me and I was curious.

"Paul," he began, "it's Bruce. Do you have a few minutes to talk?"

I was absolutely buried in work, but then I wanted it to appear to others that I had everything under control and could take time for any call that came in. So I said, "Plenty of time. Tell me what's happening with you."

He said, "I need to tell you a story, and it'll take me a little while."

"I'm all ears," I answered. The next twenty minutes led to another new chapter in my life and ministry. He began to relate the story.

Two weeks earlier, he was sitting on a platform in Portla Oregon, getting ready to speak to 2,500 teachers at one of regional meetings of the Association of Christian Schools In tional (ACSI).

"At each of these ACSI conventions," he explained, "they take up an offering for the international ministries of ACSI. Just before I was to speak, a lady by the name of Margaret Bridges came to the microphone. For the next six minutes, she gave an impassioned plea for Romania. She was so fervent and the story so compelling that half of us on the speakers' platform were in tears. I had to get my composure back before I got up to speak." The excitement in his voice was contagious.

"When she began to walk back to her seat, I motioned for her to sit next to me. As she sat down, I said to her, 'That was really a touching story. Thank you for sharing that.'

"She looked me squarely in the eyes and said, 'I believe you're supposed to get involved in Eastern Europe.'

"Afterward, when the people had left the auditorium, Mrs. Bridges was sitting down in front waiting for me. I asked her why she had asked me to go to Romania. She said that when she had been in Romania at a conference for Christian teachers, they had made her promise that if she ever saw Bruce Wilkinson she would beg him to come to Romania."

Bruce said he didn't see how he could go to Romania, but Margaret was undaunted.

"I didn't want to go either at first," she smiled. "I'm a pastor's wife and the principal of a large Christian school in Northern California.

"One Sunday evening, I watched a film on evangelism in Eastern Europe. God began to work in my heart. I repented of my own selfishness and pride. I promised God that I would be willing to go to Eastern Europe with the gospel. About this same time, I received an invitation to go to Timisoara, Romania, to help educators start a Christian school. I accepted the invitation and asked God to confirm His direction in my life.

"The following Sunday," she continued, "I was singing in the choir and saw a number of visitors in the congregation. Afterward, I came down from the choir to speak to a young couple, introduce myself as the pastor's wife, and welcome them to the church. The husband responded, 'We weren't planning to come here this morning. But as we drove by, the Lord impressed upon our hearts to turn the car around and come to this church.'

"I asked them, 'Why are you here?'

" 'We're from Romania,' they responded, 'and we would like to ask you to go to Romania. And when you go, you can stay with my parents. They have an apartment in Timisoara Square.'

"Within three days, God had moved in a very definite way to confirm my calling to Eastern Europe.

"I went to Romania, Bruce. And I believe the Lord wants you to go as well," Margaret said firmly. Bruce agreed.

As we continued to talk on the telephone, I was amazed.

"That was just the beginning, Paul," Bruce went on. "It didn't stop there. The Lord began to really work on me. About a week later Margaret called me at home. She said she felt there was something more than Romania that I and Walk Thru the Bible should be involved in. She didn't know what it was. She just had a great burden for the former Soviet Union and all of Eastern Europe.

"After she hung up, I sat down and began to pray. A little while later the Lord was convicting me, so I got up and walked into the guest bedroom. I laid flat on the floor and began to pray again. The Lord churned my emotions up and I couldn't understand what was going on. I don't remember everything I was praying, but I do remember saying, 'Lord, I recognize that You are doing something I can't explain, but I'm willing to do anything You want me to do. I'm willing, if You really want me to, to go to Romania.' And then, Paul, I began to repent.

"I wasn't repenting about sins, but for not being as open to going to the foreign field as perhaps He wanted me to be. I said, 'Lord, if You want us to move to Romania or Russia, or wherever You want us to go, I'm willing. If that means selling our house, our cars, emptying our bank accounts, leaving Walk Thru the Bible—if that's what You want, You have it.'

"Finally, I reached the point where I was begging God to send us. My repentance was pretty deep, and my tears had wet the floor by the time I got up. Then I asked myself, who needs to know this? I don't know why, but I felt that Paul Eshleman needed to know it. That's why I'm calling.

"Paul, I'm going through some things in my life, and I don't understand where they are leading. Let me tell you about one other thing I believe the Lord is burdening me about.

"About a year ago," he went on, "I felt I had plateaued in my spiritual walk with the Lord. I went away for a week with my wife, Darlene, to think about the future and to pray. I decided to take seriously the command of the Scriptures to 'number our days.'

"I began to write down some dreams for what I wanted the Lord to do in my life and ministry," he continued. "Please don't laugh, but one of my private prayers was that the Lord would someday allow me to teach the Bible to millions of people each week."

"Does it matter where those people live?" I asked.

"Not any more."

"Then there's something I have to tell you about."

For the next hour I told him about the wonderful open door we had discovered into the public schools of the Soviet Union. I told him about the tremendous need for capable teachers to lead the convocations we hoped to sponsor. I told him of my vision to send workers over to each city to follow up the convocations and help the teachers begin teaching the Christian ethics course in their classrooms. And I explained the need for Bible-teaching videos for parents in adult Christian education classes that I believed we could set up in each school. These classes could help provide a place to grow in their faith for those being reached by the big media efforts.

Bruce responded, "We'll help in any way. Let's meet."

The tears began to flow down my cheeks. I'd had such a burden that so much more needed to be done, and now God was answering my prayers. He was prompting others to get involved. I had no idea then what a big answer it would be. Bruce and I agreed to meet October 11 to talk.

But the Lord was not through pulling things together.

Three months earlier Jerry and Karen Franks had taken two of the leading officials from the Russian Ministry of Education with them to the conference of educators in Romania, sponsored by ACSI. While there, these Russian officials expressed their need for help in training their teachers in the latest educational techniques and philosophy. Since that time, the ACSI leadership had been very concerned about the need.

About an hour after Bruce and I finished talking, Dr. Paul Kienel, president of ACSI, called him. This body is made up of the largest group of Christian schools in the world and includes more than 40,000 Christian teachers.

"Bruce," Paul said, "we've been invited to the Soviet Union to help give additional training to their public school teachers. We think your organization is especially equipped to do that."

Bruce told him about the conversation he had just had with me. "Have you two ever met?" he asked.

"No, but I know who he is."

"We're planning to meet in Atlanta on October 11. You probably should come."

"Well, it's obvious that the Lord is doing something big. Let me check my datebook." And after a short pause, "On that date I'm in charge of a major convention."

"I understand," Bruce said.

"No, wait. I'm going to get out of that commitment. I'll find someone to take my place. I'll be in Atlanta."

Bruce told him that he didn't know what we were going to do. We had no agenda for that meeting.

"I understand," Paul smiled over the phone. "The Lord knows what we need to do. I'll see you there."

On October 11 I flew to Atlanta for the meeting. Curt Mackey, then director of international training for Campus Crusade for Christ, flew in from South America for the day. Paul Kienel came from California, Phil Rennicks from Alabama, and we were joined by eight key staff members of Walk Thru the Bible. We began to talk about what God was doing in the Soviet Union and Eastern Europe. We prayed about what we should do now.

I talked about the four-day convocations we were holding in the Soviet Union. We were averaging three to four hundred teachers at each one. We were taking forty to fifty North American Christians over to staff each meeting. We desperately needed additional qualified teachers and instructors for all the conferences we were to conduct.

"How can we help?" Bruce inquired eagerly.

"You could send some of your Walk Thru the Bible instructors over to help with the conferences."

"How many do you want?"

"As many as you can send."

"Okay," Bruce promised. "We'll guarantee at least eight at each convocation. How much does it cost?"

"About $3,000 per person. We go for seventeen days. We do a convocation in one city, take the weekend off to travel, and then repeat the convocation the next week in another city. We want to do 150 cities, so we will need people for 75 trips."

"Done. We will send eight people per trip for the next 75 trips. Don't think about it anymore. We will raise the money. It will happen."

Then Bruce asked me how the Christian School movement could help. I had never met Paul Kienel. When Bruce first suggested that ACSI should join us for the meeting, I was not sure why. As our time progressed together, I saw the incredible fit. This organization could provide the professional educators needed to give our convocations educational credibility. So I said, "We could use three professional Christian teachers for each of the three groups we teach—elementary, secondary, and principals. We could use nine each time."

Bruce turned to Paul Kienel. "You need to send nine each trip. Nine times 75. At $3,000 each."

Paul didn't respond immediately.

Bruce said, "Paul, you don't know Paul Eshleman. I do. I want you to know you can trust him. You know me. Take my word for it."

Paul was interested, but remained hesitant. He had to talk with his board.

Then Bruce said, "This isn't a committee. We are always getting committees together. There's always too much talk and too little action. We need to be an action group. I have to talk to my board as well. But I sense your board and my board will say yes to this. Do you want to do it?"

"I've never done anything like this before," he smiled.

"Neither have I."

"Yes, I want to do it!" Paul Kienel affirmed.

I was shaking my head in disbelief. I had never seen organizations make decisions so quickly. I had never before seen them embrace and fund a plan they didn't develop themselves.

Then I told them that I believed the biggest need in the Soviet Union was for Christians to teach the Bible. There simply weren't enough teachers or pastors, or churches, to contain the harvest and disciple all the new believers. What we needed was a good video curriculum. We thought it would take about three years to take a person who knows nothing about Christianity to the point where he could lead a group.

Bruce said, "We in Walk Thru will take the responsibility of developing up to 150 hours of video instruction and translate it into Russian. Also, as a part of our commitment, we will train 2,400 teachers to conduct Walk Thru the Bible seminars in the schools and colleges."

Pat McMillan, a management consultant and long-time friend to many of us, had joined the meeting for a few hours. He said, "I think you should call your group the CoMission. You are cooperating to help fulfill the Great Commission." We agreed.

The meeting ended and we took a picture on the front steps of the building. Those were memorable moments.

We had great enthusiasm. Would the Lord confirm our steps? Would He bring our dreams to pass?

CHAPTER 23

The Vision Expands

In the weeks that followed, God amazingly confirmed that we had embarked on something dear to His heart. At this point, our three organizations were just getting to know each other. While I was in Albania for the premiere of the "JESUS" film, the Lord confirmed the involvement in the Soviet Union to both Bruce Wilkinson and Paul Kienel.

We needed God to confirm to each of us individually that it was His plan for us to work together in this undertaking and that He was orchestrating it.

In the days to come we would be filled with confirmations beyond what any of us had ever imagined. The initial experience with the "JESUS" film in the Soviet Union was a personal story, but through the CoMission, God was about to do things that would unleash an avalanche of stories from everyone involved.

Bruce Wilkinson took a major leadership role, and I encouraged him to go as soon as possible and attend a convocation so he could see the possibilities in Russia for himself.

He left a few weeks later on his first trip to the Soviet Union.

"A miracle happened in those four days," he reported. "We began to see that God really had opened a door so large, and the field was so incredibly ripe, that we didn't know what to do with it.

"I remember a staff prayer meeting I was leading for our group on Thursday morning at 6:30, before we began the first session of the day.

"Forty of us gathered together. After a short Bible reading, we broke into groups of three or four as I led us in fervent prayer for the Russian people. It was a moving time. And then I said, 'I want you to tell the Lord that if He wants to move you to Russia, you'll go.' Silence. You could have heard a pin drop. No one said a word.

"'If we cannot pray that way,' I continued, 'and there are conditions to our obedience to Christ, the anointing of God will be hindered, and it will stop. There must be no hindrances. If God says do it, our reaction must be: Where, and when, and how do I do it?'

"People began to pray. Throughout that hour of prayer, it became obvious that thousands of people needed to move to the Soviet Union. It was the biggest open door to the gospel that the Christian church had ever seen. It really was. And we began to pray for thousands of people to go to Russia."

One of the men in the meeting was Bart Trowbridge. He painted a graphic word-picture of the opportunity. "When I think of the Soviet Union, I compare it to a great orchard of fruit. The branches are so full that they almost touch the ground. In the middle of the night a wind blows through and knocks the fruit off and it covers the ground. The next morning we go out to see the orchard. We all stand there with our arms crossed saying, 'Boy, look at that. Someone should go in and pick up all that fruit.'"

We scheduled another CoMission meeting in January. Paul Kienel agreed to host the meeting at the ACSI headquarters in La Habra, California. When Bruce asked what I thought about inviting other organizations to join us, I readily agreed.

The meeting opened on Thursday morning, January 23, 1992, with twenty-two ministries represented. Most of the attendees were presidents or held key leadership roles in their organizations. Among those attending were the presidents of Moody Bible Institute, Biola University, Child Evangelism Fellowship, and Worldteam. Leaders from Slavic Gospel, Focus on the Family, Multnomah Bible School, Columbia Bible College, U.S. Center for World Missions, and many others also attended.

The goal of the meeting was to join together in a way that Christian leaders never had before. Typically, we compete. Sometimes we cooperate. This usually just means that I do my thing and you do your thing, and we don't get in each other's way. We've never come together as an army, to make it happen *together*, to make God's work one.

The biggest challenge was whether or not this was really possible. If this open door proved to be the largest in the history of the church, then this was the time we had to attempt that cohesion.

The first morning, Bruce Wilkinson led the meeting. "By the time this meeting is over," he said, "we'll know if God is in this or not. No one will have to tell us. We'll all leave saying, 'God did it' or 'He didn't.'"

So the goal became the development of a brand new vision that none of us had exclusively, that no one of us owned. It had to be one where no one could say, "That's my vision. Come help me do my thing." Every one of us must say, "This is our vision. We're going to do it *together.*"

The Thursday meeting was somewhat frustrating. Several people had already heard about the convocations and about some of the ideas we had. They kept asking, "What is the plan? What's the strategy? How are we going to do it?"

Another small group appeared skeptical. They seemed to say, "I know you're going to lay some plan on us at any moment, and I am prepared to tell you what is wrong with it. And no matter what you say, I probably will be against it."

Yet another group of people just wanted to know how they might fit into whatever was ultimately decided.

"Don't worry about the plan," Bruce kept saying. "If we work on a plan, what will happen if the plan doesn't work? We'll all quit and say God wasn't in it. Plans change. It can't be a plan. It can't be a strategy. It has to be God doing something in our hearts, so that if the plan doesn't work, or the strategy fails, we still keep going."

We broke for the evening. Bruce and I sat in his room from 9:30 until 1:30 in the morning talking and praying and trying to figure out what to do. We didn't know.

The next morning we looked at the pattern of Nehemiah when he went back to Jerusalem to rebuild the wall that had broken down. Before he went back, he repented of his own sin.

As Bruce again led the meeting on Friday, he began, "In the past, sin is what has stopped Christian leaders like ourselves from working together. That's why we haven't done it. It's the will of God that we do this so the world may see that we are one, and right now we're not one. What are the sins that have stopped us from working together?"

He went to the blackboard and began to list them as they were called out from around the table. He filled a whole board. Arrogance. Independence. Pride. Love of money. Love of power. Ego-centeredness. Turfdom. Afraid someone will steal our donors. On and on. The room became quiet, and the quiet was sobering.

"What we have to do now is repent," Bruce suggested. "Repentance is not a feeling; it is a choice. We choose to repent. I don't want you to close your eyes. I want you to look at that list on the board and pick out one that convicts you. I want you to confess it on your own behalf and then on behalf of all of us. We're all guilty of many of these to a greater or lesser extent."

It was hard at first. Some perfunctory prayers were prayed. Then one man began to weep as he asked God to forgive him for his pride and arrogance—and repentance came like a flood over the room. There were no dry eyes.

When the repentance was completed, we turned back to the example of Nehemiah. He had a burden.

Bruce cleaned off the board and we started again. We asked what the burdens of the Soviet people were. We asked how they were feeling at this time. It was not difficult to imagine. They felt betrayed. Their dream was gone. They felt lied to and embarrassed. They were not a world-class power. Their economy was in shambles. Most of all, they had to be feeling hopeless. We asked God to allow us to feel, just a little bit, what the Soviets must be feeling at this point in their history. We asked God to give us a little of their burdens.

Then Bruce erased the board again and asked how God felt about the Soviets. He loves them. He is not willing that any should perish, but that they all should come to repentance. He sent Jesus to die for them. He cares. He grieves. He forgives. He keeps seeking.

Then we asked God to put His burden on our hearts. We prayed and the peace of God began to fill us.

But several men in the room said they just felt overwhelmed. "When I look at the size of the Soviet Union," one said, "I feel like we can't do it at all. I feel like it's a black hole and no matter how many resources we pour into it, we won't get anywhere."

"But when God looks at the task," Bruce interjected, "is He overwhelmed with it?"

"No."

"Whenever we have our eyes focused on the task, we'll always feel overwhelmed. Tell me a couple of things God has done in the Old and New Testaments that will make this task look like nothing." The answers flew quickly from the floor.

"He created the world."

"He raised Christ from the dead."

"He led the Israelites across the Red Sea."

"He fed two million people in the wilderness."

Each time somebody else said something, God grew larger in our eyes. We forgot about the task and started focusing on God. When we saw the task through His eyes, our faith grew and our fear disappeared.

We prayed again. We acknowledged on the basis of His omniscience and His omnipotence that this was not a big thing to Him. At this point we were ready to work.

As we broke for lunch, Paul Kienel, Bruce, and I sat at a separate table.

"What do you think we should do now?" Bruce wondered.

I said, "I think we should ask them to send people over as workers for at least a year."

Bruce turned to Paul Kienel. "How many workers could ACSI send over next year?"

Paul said, "I think we could send a hundred couples a year for the next five years."

If we could conduct convocations in 150 cities, we would need 150 teams of ten to follow them up. We would need 1,500 people to go. When the meeting resumed after lunch, we challenged those who were there to make a commitment about how many they would send. We encouraged them not to give any number unless the Lord was prompting them.

We began to total them on the board.

"ACSI pledges 200," from Paul Kienel.

"Child Evangelism Fellowship pledges 75."

"Walk Thru the Bible pledges 100."

"Worldteam pledges 10."

"Slavic Gospel pledges 40."

"Campus Crusade for Christ will try to send 240."

"Moody pledges 100."

Bruce interrupted his good friend, Joe Stowell. "Joe, don't forget that you have *Moody* magazine and the radio network."

Joe said, "You're right. Moody pledges 100 students, and another 300 a year from the community at large."

And so it went. When we totaled it up a few minutes later, the organizations had committed to sending 1,280 people.

A few weeks later, the Navigators, who had been unable to attend the meeting, unanimously voted to send 400 a year for five years.

We checked with missions experts, and none could recall any time in the history of the church where more than 800 missionaries had been sent out in one year. We would have to see what would happen.

CHAPTER 24

The CoMission
Launches Out

The next meeting of the CoMission convened on the evening of March 30. It was held in an upstairs classroom in the new Moody Center for Evangelism. As usual, we began by tracing the origins of the united vision and the fact that none of us currently involved had set out to organize some new thing. The next morning when we went to the time of confession, it was a much larger group.

Bill Bright sat on the front row. John Corts, president of the Billy Graham Association, sat in the back on the left. Bill Gothard was seated near the front. Many other presidents of organizations and Christian colleges were also in attendance.

By the afternoon, we realized that things were not going well.

Several men arrived late, missing the time of personal confession. When it came time to discuss the strategy, they vehemently opposed the course of action agreed on in the LaHabra meeting. They felt that everything needed to be done in and through the existing local church in the Soviet Union. They also felt that our stated objectives for the movement had to be church-planting.

It was discouraging. I got up and explained that I had met with the church leaders in Russia, and they had encouraged us to go ahead. They had told me that the Communists had not allowed them to go to college or seminary. Thus, they lacked the credibility necessary to work within the educational system.

In my meeting with Gregori Komendant, president of the Evangelical-Baptist Federation, he had simply asked that we make the same materials we were giving to secular school teachers available to the churches. And he asked that we devote time to the preparation of indigenous Russian leadership. I agreed that we would do both.

We were at an impasse. Some of the men were ready to walk out.

Bruce Wilkinson, who was leading the meeting at the time, said, "I don't know what the Lord would have us do. If the Lord is impressing one of you with a direction for us, please come up and speak." He put down the chalk with which he had been listing ideas on the blackboard and took a seat in the audience.

No one was leading the meeting.

Then Andrew Semenchuk, a long-time veteran of the Slavic Gospel Association and now of Russian Ministries, got up and slowly walked to the podium in front. He was a big, bearish man with a deep voice and a warm smile.

"About seventy years ago," he began, "just after the Bolshevik Revolution, Russia was open briefly to the gospel. On this very block where we are meeting today, a group of mission leaders met to discuss the idea of working together to send missionaries to Russia. The meetings ended with no agreement, and the workers were not sent. Gentleman, we cannot let that happen again."

Then Jerry Franks, who was seated in the second row, opened his Bible and read the passage from Acts 16:9,10:

During the night Paul had a vision of a man of Macedonia standing and begging him. "Come over to Macedonia and help us." After Paul had seen the vision, we got ready at once to leave for Macedonia, concluding that God had called us to preach the gospel to them.

"I believe that's the situation we're in right now," Jerry observed, "except we haven't needed a vision. We have been to Russia, and they have personally begged us to come. I believe our only choice is to do what Paul did: get ready to go at once, because we conclude that God is calling us to go."

It was a turning point. We realized that not everyone might join in the CoMission. That was sad, and we began a series of side meetings to resolve some of those differences. But we could not allow ourselves to be deterred by those who were not in favor of our course of action. We needed to get moving. And eventually more than eighty organizations joined the movement.[1]

---

[1] These organizations are listed at the end of this chapter.

In the next day and a half, the fastest organizational developments took place that I have ever seen in my life. We divided those at the meeting into working committees that would develop all the policies and procedures which we would all abide by as a part of working together. Our original executive committee was expanded.

Paul Kienel headed up the school curriculum committee and began developing a plan to help the Russians rewrite their textbooks and to provide additional training for their teachers.

Paul Johnson, a businessman from Detroit, headed up the arrangements committee, which was charged with finding the housing and equipment needed for all the CoMissioners who would move overseas.

In the weeks that followed, others were added: John Kyle, president of Mission to the World, headed up mobilization. How could we recruit thousands of people to move to the Soviet Union for a year?

Dr. Terry Taylor, U.S. president for the Navigators, took over the training and materials committee. They would decide how the CoMissioners would be trained and what materials would be used.

Peter Deyneka, president of Russian Ministries, would be our liaison with everything going on in the Soviet Union. Mary Lance Sisk, a businesswomen from Charlotte, North Carolina, headed up our prayer effort. Dr. Joe Stowell, president of Moody Bible Institute, coordinated our relations with the Russian Church.

J. B. Crouse, president of OMS International, was in charge of other countries who wanted to cooperate in sending people to work with the CoMission in the Soviet Union.

Margaret Bridges and Ralph Plumb, president of International Aid, joined later to handle new projects of the CoMission.

I served as vice-chairman of the executive committee and headed up the sending organizations committee. We were to determine how all the workers would actually get over there.

During the next thirty-six hours, a host of decisions were made. None of us believed the door of opportunity in the Soviet Union would stay open long; therefore, we realized we'd better not quibble about policies and procedures. We'd better just get on with the task as quickly as possible.

*CoMission Executive Committee (left to right): (standing) Peter Deyneka Jr.,
J. B. Crouse, Paul Johnson, Joe Stowell, John Kyle, Terry Taylor;
(seated) Paul Kienel, Bruce Wilkinson, Paul Eshleman.
Not pictured: Ralph Plumb, Mary Lance Sisk, and Margaret Bridges.*

We decided that all workers would go out under fifteen or so sending organizations that had previous experience in recruiting, training, and supervising missionaries overseas.

By the end of the thirty-six hours, we had passed sixty-five recommendations for policies. These were accepted by the executive committee, and we left with assignments made to get the recruiting under way.

If we were going to get people sent over in the fall, they would have to be recruited, processed, and approved; they would have to raise their support, be trained and moved over, have apartments found, and interpreters recruited—all in five months.

In the next twelve months, I would speak twenty-eight times to more than 8,000 people, challenging them to go to Russia. I began each talk with the same simple challenge. "At the end of this meeting, I'm going to ask you to quit your job and move to the former Soviet Union for a year to help disciple the teachers who are waiting for you to come. I'll have a piece of paper here in the front for you to sign if you are willing to go."

People began to respond. By October, the first two teams of ten people had been recruited and were on their way to Moscow and St. Petersburg. By the next summer, the number had grown to more than three hundred. When I walked into the training sessions at Olivet Nazarene College outside Chicago, I was greeted by many I had met along the road.

A team of six from Rolling Hills Covenant Church in California, whom I had recruited to go, were going out under the Navigators. Six came from Fellowship Bible Church in Little Rock, Arkansas. Several had come from Briarwood Presbyterian in Birmingham, Alabama. Some from Campus Crusade meetings. And five from South Coast Community Church in Irvine, California.

One of the men came up to talk with me. "I'm sure you don't remember, but when you spoke to the men's breakfast at South Coast, you said that if someone was out of a job at present, maybe God was freeing him up to go to Russia for a year. Then you looked right at me. Well, I was out of a job. And I don't know if I'd have been willing to go if God hadn't gotten my attention. So I'm on my way now, and I wanted to say thanks."

The word about the CoMission was getting out, and the stories that came back to us had one common thread. "God is in this! There's just no other way to explain it!"

The first training session for the CoMission candidates was held at the Navigators headquarters in Glen Eyrie, Colorado. One night after dinner, Terry Taylor and I sat down with the two teams who were getting ready to leave for Moscow to tell them how much we appreciated their courage and commitment.

"You will be the pioneers," we said. "No one has ever done what we are asking you to do. The strategy is untested. We are eager to see and hear what you learn."

Then we took some time to hear from them about how the Lord had brought in their finances. One of the first to speak was a young woman who had been doubtful that she could raise the funds.

"By the time I got my acceptance," she began, "I had already committed myself to counsel at a youth camp. That meant I would have only four weeks to raise my support. I'd have to raise $5,000 each week. But I decided that if God was really in this, He could do it. So I did what they told me in the training. I sent out letters to everyone I knew and started making phone calls. All the money came in and I have $1,000 more than I need."

The next story was similar. Two sisters from the same family wanted to go. They both knew the same people. Between them, they would have to raise more than $40,000. But they also sent out their letters. They also had a surplus.

Tom, one of the team leaders, was the next to speak. "Our situation was totally different. We didn't think we were going to make it this time. We thought we'd probably have to wait for the next group going over and join them.

"A close friend of ours came by the house to say hello before he returned to Hong Kong. We told him about our desire to go with the CoMission. As he was leaving he asked me to give him my last promotional video. I was really reluctant, but he pressed, so I gave it to him. A few days later, he called from Hong Kong and asked if we had our bags packed. I told him no because we still needed about $8,000. He said we'd better start packing because he had shown the video to some of his friends in Hong Kong and they were putting the $8,000 in the mail to us. It's just a miracle of God."

"So was our situation," another couple broke in. "We knew we couldn't go on the CoMission unless we sold our home. We couldn't afford to make the house payments while we were gone. The training here started on a Sunday, so we knew that we had to have it sold by the Friday before we left. On Friday afternoon, a couple who had looked at the house earlier called to say that they would buy it if we could guarantee that they would get the financing from the bank."

"We called the bank," the husband said, "and asked to speak to the loan officer. Both the head loan officer and the assistant loan officer had taken an early weekend. I asked for their home phone numbers. The head loan officer didn't answer, but I finally reached the assistant loan officer on her car phone. She was stopped at a red light.

"We told her our problem and she said she would like to help us but the head loan officer really had to give the final approval. We were just about to hang up when she said, 'Wait a minute. He just pulled up beside me here at the light.' Well, they pulled their cars over to the side of the road. He approved the loan over the phone, and here we are. God did it!"

Meanwhile, the effort to expand the convocations to more cities was moving full-speed ahead. The office group in Moscow grew to twenty-five. We hired Russians to help with the negotiations in each city. We needed to send in the American representatives to sign the contracts, but after the initial contacts were made, it was our Russian staff who knew what we really should pay for everything.

There was so much to do. Secure housing for the sixty-five people coming in to operate each four-day convocation. Make sure that buses, drivers, and meal schedules were coordinated. Check to see if they had enough meat for the week to feed our group. Hire fifty interpreters for the small groups. Arrange for the break-out rooms for the various seminars. Build the simultaneous interpreter booths for the plenary sessions. Find a secure place for the tons of materials that would be shipped in.

In addition, we had to make sure that all key Communist Party officials were notified, and that things were coordinated among the city officials, the regional Ministry of Education, and the city Ministry of Education. In the early days, so few Americans had been to some of the cities that our arrival had to be handled with much of the same ceremony and preparation as an official diplomatic mission.

We opened an office in Leningrad. Lauren Bloom, Nils and Sandy Becker, and eventually a host of others moved to Moscow to assist in setting up and conducting the convocations.

At a family reunion, I challenged my brother-in-law, Don Hawblitzel, and his wife, Nancy, to go to Moscow to help with the tremendous logistical problems. Within months they sold their business, sold their house, raised their support, and moved to Russia. Don established a warehouse for gathering and packaging the more than 60,000 pieces of literature that we shipped to each convocation. Nancy handled some of the never-ending administrative and financial details. Together, they helped handle the logistics for some of the conferences in the Ukraine.

As I sat talking with them in their little apartment in Moscow, their faces shone radiantly and their hearts overflowed with what they had been privileged to see and do for the Lord.

"We were nearing the semi-retirement milestone," he said, "just getting ready to take it a little easier, spend some time with the grandkids, and that kind of thing. Now I feel as though we've stepped on a springboard to a ministry beyond what we ever thought possible. We are involved in the most significant and meaningful ministry of our lives."

I wondered how many other "empty nesters" like them could be as greatly used of the Lord if they would just take the first step. I thought of a message I heard once. The speaker said, "Moses never would have left Egypt if he'd had to solve the Red Sea problem first. It's our job to make the decision to go. It's God's job to part the sea."

As we set up in one city, incredible reports poured in. The response continued to be almost unbelievable from convocations being held all across Siberia.

In Magadan, a city about four hours flight from Alaska, the team saw pictures depicting remains from some of the most brutal prison camps in all of Russia. In one camp, hundreds of Christian pastors had been brutally killed for their faith. Almost everyone was a descendant of someone who had been in a camp or had been one of the guards of a camp. Their memories indicated the crucial need for reconciliation, for a new start. The lesson on forgiveness seemed too good to be true.

All the lessons in the course taught the benefit to society of this moral foundational truth: When people practice forgiveness, the cycle of revenge is broken.

One of the most exciting reports came from Blagoveshchensk, down on the border with China. At the end of the convocation, the mayor of the city came to speak to the group of sixty Americans who had been conducting the sessions.

"I would like to make a request of you," he began. "We would like you to leave a picture of yourself, and any memento of your family with us. We would like to start a display in our museum in your honor. You see, the name of our city, Blagoveshchensk, means 'the gospel.' And we would like to honor you who brought the gospel back to us after fifty years."

The mail brought still more requests to conduct convocations in other cities, but we needed to see what progress was being made in cities where we had already been. We sent out a questionnaire, and more than 1,300 teachers responded; 71 percent had already shown the "JESUS" video or film. The ones who hadn't said they didn't have access to a VCR. But 93 percent said they were teaching the course, and 96 percent were reading the Bible regularly and discussing it in their classes.

Larissa, a teacher in Vologda, teaches her class a lesson on kindness.

Several leaders went back to Vologda to see what was happening with the teachers who had taken the course there, and how we could better prepare them in the convocation to teach the Christian Ethics and Morality course.

When they arrived at one of the local schools, Jerry Franks asked if anyone was presenting the course there. He was told that a teacher named Larissa was teaching it, and if they wished, they could join the class. Larissa had not attended the convocation, but she had taken the materials brought back by the principal. This day she would teach the second graders.

In honor of the guests, Larissa asked the children to stand and sing a song they had learned with one of the "Praise and Worship" tapes distributed at the convocation. The children stood by their desks, freshly scrubbed and neatly dressed in their black and white uniforms, and began to sing, "Jesus, name above all names, beautiful Savior, glorious Lord..." [2]

Then it was time for the lesson, which today was on kindness.

---

[2] "Jesus Name Above All Names" words and music by Naida Hearn. © 1974 Scripture in Song (administered by Maranatha! Music in care of The Copyright Company, Nashville, Tennessee). All rights reserved. International copyright secured. Used by permission.

"Is it easy or difficult to be kind?" Larissa asked the class.

"Oh, it's very hard," they chorused back.

"Why is that?"

"Because people aren't kind back."

"Was Jesus kind to people?" Larissa asked. The whole class had watched the "JESUS" film several times.

"Yes, He was kind," they answered. "He was even kind to the people who killed Him."

"Do we need to tell other people about it when we are kind to someone?" Larissa pushed the point a little further.

"No. Jesus healed people and then He told them not to tell anyone," came the answer. "So we can be kind to people and no one needs to know."

"Why did Jesus heal the daughter of Jairus?" Larissa continued her questioning.

A little girl in the front of the room, with a crisp white bow in her hair, raised her hand. "Because He promised her father that everything would be all right, and Jesus can't lie, so He had to heal his daughter."

Pictures from the "JESUS" film help Larissa teach a variety of Bible stories.

At the side of the room, a little boy gestured frantically, hoping to get a chance at the question. In Russian classrooms there are rules for how a child raises his or her hand. He places his left hand on the desk, palm up, holding his right elbow. This makes about thirty kids look like they are doing karate chops, trying to get the teacher's attention.

Larissa selected the boy at the side. "Jesus raised the daughter of Jairus because we're all supposed to tell people about Jesus," he said, "and she couldn't tell anybody because she was dead."

Teachers from five other schools, who had come to see how to teach the course, sat in the back of the room, eager to learn. They asked, "Couldn't you send us someone to help us also learn to teach this course?"

The CoMission was desperately needed.

November 5, just thirteen months after our initial meeting, we took the official public relations launch of the CoMission to the regional meeting of ACSI at the Anaheim Convention Center. About 8,000 Christian school teachers attended.

In an impressive opening ceremony, officials from the Russian Ministry of Education strode into the arena behind marching bands and waving flags. They received a standing ovation.

With her arms open wide, Dr. Olga Polykovskaya invited the teachers to come and help them. "We need you. We want you. We will welcome you and your Christian ideals to our country, to our schools, and to our hearts."

A national press conference immediately after the opening session brought reporters from all the major wire services and national news magazines. At one point, someone asked Dr. Asmolov, the deputy minister of education, why he would get involved with a religious group that didn't seem to represent all the mainline denominations.

Asmolov answered brilliantly. "When a man is drowning under a waterfall, and a hand is reached out to him, does he ask,

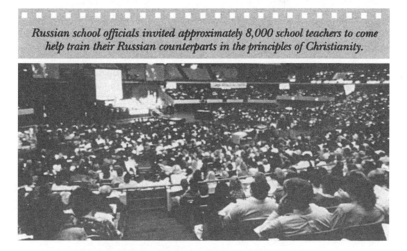

Russian school officials invited approximately 8,000 school teachers to come help train their Russian counterparts in the principles of Christianity.

'Whose hand is this?' The CoMission was the first hand to reach out to us to help provide moral teaching for our schools, and we intend to take that hand."

The CoMission would face great challenges in the months ahead. Most of the leadership involved would face opposition from their own organizations over the amount of money and manpower being invested in one area of the world.

Despite difficulties, those of us on the executive committee felt that we simply had to stay together. As Christian leaders, we had to learn to work together, both for the cause of the kingdom and as an example of how others could work together in fulfilling the Great Commission. And God was bringing the people.

CoMission members (sending organizations are shown in italics): A.C.M.C. (Association of Church Missions Committee), Alpha Care Therapy Services, American Tract Society, Association of Christian Schools International, Baptist General Conference, *BCM International*, B.E.E. International, Biola University, BMC International, BMC of USA, Boneem International, Bright Hope International, *Campus Crusade for Christ*, Campus Outreach Augusta, Cedarville College, Child Evangelism Fellowship, Chosen People Ministries, *The Christian and Missionary Alliance*, Christian Associates International, The Christian Bridge, Church Resources Ministries, Columbia International University, Community Bible Study, Daniel Iverson Center for Christian Studies, Educational Services International, *European Christian Mission*, Evangelical Covenant Church, Evangelical Free Church Mission, Evangelical Friends Mission, Evangelical Mennonite Church, Evangelical Methodist World Missions, Evangelism Explosion III International, Fellowship of Evangelical Bible Churches, Focus on the Family, Foreign Mission Board of the Southern Baptist Convention, Gospel Light Publications, *Gospel Missionary Union*, Grace College of the Bible (Nebraska), Great Commission Ministries, HCJB World Radio, In Touch Ministries, Institute for East/West Christian Studies, Wheaton College, International Aid, Inc., International Coalition for Christian Counseling, International Cooperating Ministries, International Teams, John Guest Evangelistic Team, Lancaster Bible College, Maranatha Ministries International, Mission Athletes International, Mission Aviation Fellowship, *The Mission Society for United Methodists, Mission to the World*, Mission to Unreached Peoples, Missionary Board of the Church of God (Anderson, Indiana), Missions Fest Vancouver, Moody Bible Institute, Multnomah School of the Bible, Nashville Bible College, *The Navigators, OMS International*, Philadelphia College of the Bible, Prairie Bible Institute, Project C.A.R.E. (Coordination of All Resources for Evangelism), Reimer Foundation, Ronald Blue & Company, Russian Ministries, Salt and Light, Sea-Tac Ministries, *SEND International*, Serve International, Slavic Gospel Association, Team Expansion, Transport for Christ, U.S. Center for World Missions, Walk Thru the Bible Ministries, *Wesleyan World Missions*, World Gospel Mission, World Help, World Partners, *Worldteam*.

CHAPTER 25

The Greatest Promise

People came from every walk of life. By the third year, more than nine hundred were already serving the Lord through the CoMission in countries of the former Soviet Union. Hundreds were in the process of submitting their applications. Thousands of teachers were being discipled in forty cities. As I visited the teams, I was overcome by God's answer to prayer.

I visited with Kurt and Elke Kiesling, who were leading the team in Dnepropotrovsk, Ukraine. A young Southern California youth pastor with a surfer's tan, an infectious grin, and an easygoing manner, Kurt made me think that he had all the time in the world just to talk to me.

"This has been the greatest year of our lives." His enthusiasm overflowed. "Obviously, receiving Christ was the most important thing that ever happened to me. But this year I have changed and grown more, spiritually and mentally, than in any other year of my life.

"We have seen the Lord use us not only to follow up on the teachers who were reached through the convocation, but also to help develop those teachers into spiritual leaders for their country. Their impact will last long after we have returned to the U.S."

His main goal in the CoMission was to raise up national leaders who would run their own Bible studies, train teachers in other schools in how to teach the Christian Ethics and Morality course, and be able to lead and develop Bible studies in the community for parents.

"We have seen these things take place," Kurt beamed. "A lot of people have come to know Christ this year, but even more exciting, we have found twelve to fourteen leaders who will be able to pick up the ministry and run with it."

Dnepropotrovsk had been a "closed" city for seventy years. Foreigners were banned from traveling there because it was the location of the factories that manufactured parts for nuclear bombs, nuclear submarines, and the aerospace industry. At one time, 250,000 people worked in one factory. But now the cold war has ended; the factory walls are crumbling, and the people are out of work. The economic future is not bright. The long lines at the vodka stores on Karl Marx Street comprise one more tribute to the empty lives left in the collapse of the Marxist dream.

When Kurt and Elke and their team arrived, they were treated almost as heroes. They were the first Westerners ever to set foot on the campuses where they worked. Elke appeared several times on the local television news and interview shows to explain what they were doing in the city and how people could live by the moral and ethical teachings of Jesus, taken from the Bible.

During the day, in various schools, they held classes for teachers on how to teach the morals and ethics course. At other times, they held Bible studies so these same teachers could grow in their own personal faith. In the evenings, they showed the "JESUS" film to parents, and began follow-up Bible studies in the parents' homes.

It was not an easy assignment; they had left a lot of conveniences behind. They were in a city with no mall, no shopping centers, no McDonald's or Pizza Hut. No supermarkets, cleaners, or laundromats. And they lived in a tiny apartment where they rejoiced when the elevator worked and the water ran hot. But those things didn't seem to matter.

"What stands out in your mind about your year in the Ukraine?" I asked Elke. She was a fresh-faced, freckled blond, bursting with energy and an enthusiasm as contagious as her smile. It was no wonder she was immediately recognized as an American wherever they went. In fact, one day I asked a Russian how they can spot Americans so easily, especially since our clothing was indistinguishable. "It's in your faces," they said. "You are always smiling, and you look like you are at peace with life."

Elke was a great example.

"I will never forget the people I have worked with," she smiled nostalgically in answer to my question, "or the changes I have seen take place in their lives as they come to know the Lord."

In one of the schools Elke worked in, about four weeks into the class, a new teacher showed up. Elke introduced herself and learned that she had traveled seven hours from a different school to be in this school because she heard about our class.

"I handed her a copy of every resource we had—the curriculum, the Josh McDowell books on the resurrection, and, finally, a Bible. She started to weep. She said this was the first time she had ever held a Bible in her hands, and she didn't know what to say.

"Week after week, the teacher traveled the seven hours in the morning to get there, stayed for our hour-and-a-half class, and then traveled the seven hours back to her home. I asked her what she was doing with the information and the knowledge that she was gaining. She said she was going back to her school on Mondays and teaching those things to the other teachers there."

Eventually, Elke and Kurt visited her school and showed Bill Bright's video, *A Man Without Equal.* The response was wonderful, and she is continuing to teach the Bible to those who have responded.

"I have never seen people so hungry to know God," Elke continued. "One day during a Bible study at another school, a teacher I hadn't seen before walked in. He was a part-time coach at the school. He had heard about the Bible study so he just came in to listen.

"Afterward, he asked me through my interpreter if I could stay for awhile so he could ask some questions. I agreed, and he began, 'How can I know Christ in a personal way? How can Christ forgive my sins?' So I read through the *Four Spiritual Laws* booklet with him, and he prayed to receive Christ. He continued to come to the Bible study week after week."

"So many wonderful things happen every day," Kurt broke in. "It's tough to keep track of them all. Our team of ten has worked with nearly three hundred teachers this year. Some received Christ at the convocation, some in our Bible studies, and some as we have talked personally."

Scores of these converts are teaching the curriculum in the public schools. Some of them now teach Sunday school. "One of our great joys is to watch these teachers succeed," Kurt enthused, "We see the excitement and satisfaction in their eyes when they come back and tell us that they have just taught the parable of the prodigal son to their students and the students loved it."

One eighth-grade English class invited one of Kurt's team members to talk about life in America. When he finished, he was bombarded with a number of questions such as, "Have you been to Disneyland?" and "Have you ever met Michael Jordan?" Then someone asked him about his Christian beliefs. He spent about five minutes telling why he was a Christian, how he became a Christian, how they could become Christians, and why the CoMission team had come to their city.

After the team member left, the class asked the teacher if they could meet alone as a class for a few minutes. They talked among themselves for about fifteen minutes and then brought the teacher back into the room.

"They told her, 'We have made a decision as a class. We want to follow Christ. We want to start having a Bible study. Will you teach us?'

"So the teacher came back to our team and said, 'My class wants to have Bible study with me. How do I teach them? Will you help me?'"

The opportunities are enormous. Kurt and Elke could use five times as many people right now. That's how great the need is. "One of the heart-breaking parts of this CoMission ministry is realizing that we can't meet all the needs we see," Kurt sighed. "We actually have to tell people we have so many commitments that we cannot help them to understand the Bible. Can you imagine what it's like to tell people that? The need is incredible."

"What about the response of the students?" I asked Kurt.

"We see the students a lot when we show the 'JESUS' film. It's part of the curriculum, so we have helped the teachers show it to tens of thousands of students this year. When they see the film, they are deeply moved. They are in awe of what Jesus has done for them. It's so touching to see them bow in prayer and receive Christ as their Savior.

"They also love *The Greatest Promise* booklet, which has pictures from the film. It shows them how to receive Christ as their Savior, and explains the great promise God gives that they can then live with Him in heaven forever."

School children throughout Russia study The Greatest Promise *booklet to understand how Jesus died to forgive their sins. Pictures in the booklet are taken from the "JESUS" film.*

One day when Kurt and his team held a new teacher training class, they explained the various materials they would use through the next eight or ten weeks. One of them was *The Greatest Promise* booklet. "We gave each teacher a hundred or so booklets in addition to the Bibles, curriculum, and reference books," Kurt said. "Well, we were not prepared for what happened."

When they returned to that school several days later, they were greeted by 150 laughing, screaming kids, waving these little booklets. "The teachers hadn't waited for us to show them how to use it. They had already read through it with their students, and the students were asking us to autograph their booklets."

On the last page of the booklet is a place for the students to sign their own name and the date they prayed to ask Christ into their lives. "The students showed us they had signed that page and had received Christ. We began to talk with them through our translators and ask them where Christ is right now. With big smiles, they responded, 'He's in my heart! He's in my heart!' More than a hundred kids in just one school—it's amazing!" he marveled.

"Of course, our interpreters hear the message over and over when they translate for us. We also have seen every one of them receive Christ this year."

The experiences of Kurt and Elke were repeated in Vladimir. OMS International has done a fabulous job in that city and in a number of others. The Navigators were in St. Petersburg, Magadan, Khabarovsk, and fifteen other cities. The Christian and Missionary Alliance teams were in Odessa and the Crimea. Campus Crusade for Christ had ten teams spread from Novosibirsk to Kiev. The original vision was becoming a reality.

The OMS International CoMission team in Vladimir. These lay men and women have given a year of their lives to help disciple school teachers and assist them in showing the film to parents and starting Bible studies. Through CoMission efforts, 110,000 students saw the "JESUS" film in the first year.

God was at work. He was touching the lives of individuals in scores of cities. Nowhere was this more evident than in Stavropol, Russia. In the 1930s, Stalin ordered a purge of all Bibles and all believers. In Stavropol, this order was carried out with a vengeance. Thousands of Bibles were confiscated and multitudes of believers were sent to the gulags—prison camps—where most died for being "enemies of the state."

The CoMission sent a team to Stavropol. This city's history wasn't known at the time. But when our team had difficulty getting Bibles shipped from Moscow, someone mentioned the existence of a warehouse outside of town where Bibles had been stored since Stalin's day.

After much prayer by the team, one member finally got up the courage to go to the warehouse and ask the officials if the Bibles were still there. Sure enough, they were.

Then the Comissioners asked if they could remove the Bibles and distribute them to the people of Stavropol. The answer was "Yes!"

The next day, the CoMission team returned with a truck and several Russian workers to help load the Bibles. One helper was a young man—a skeptical, hostile, agnostic collegian who had come only for the day's wages.

As the Bibles were being loaded, one team member noticed that the young man had disappeared. Eventually, they found him in a corner of the warehouse, weeping. He had slipped away, hoping to take a Bible for himself. What he found shook him to the core.

When he opened the Bible to the inside page, he saw the handwritten signature of his grandmother! It had been her personal Bible! Out of the thousands of Bibles still in that warehouse, he stole the one belonging to his grandmother—a woman persecuted for her faith all of her life.

No wonder he was weeping—God was real! No doubt his grandmother had prayed for him and for her city. His discovery of this Bible was only a glimpse into the spiritual realm—and this young man is now being transformed by the very Bible his grandmother found so dear.

Experiences such as this are happening all over the Soviet Union. God is doing the amazing on a regular basis, making Himself known and real in thousands of lives.

In Vladimir, it was easy to see the impact that the CoMission had made. Berry and Lois Johnson and Bob and Sally Feldman were leading the teams. I spent the day going to schools in which the Feldmans were working.

We walked into an eighth-grade classroom in School 9 where the students sat two to a table. It resembled classrooms I had seen in every other city. The Russians wasted no money on new architectural ideas. It seemed that every school everywhere had been built from the same plans. I noticed that the formerly requisite picture of Lenin had been taken down. With no money to buy new pictures, a poster had taken its place.

"This class starts the curriculum today," Sally whispered to me as we took our seats at a vacant table in the back of the room. "The lesson is the Uniqueness of Jesus."

"When did this teacher become a Christian?" I asked.

"Her name is Lubov, and she became a Christian about two and a half months ago. She is very nervous because you came today; she feels that she knows so little."

I settled back in my chair. In the two years that we had been working on the Christian Ethics and Morality curriculum, this would be the first time I actually saw it taught in a Russian classroom.

Lubov began, "All of us are unique people, different in many ways." They then went through a little exercise to see how they were unique, underlining the point that God had created each of us individually.

Then she switched to the spiritual study. "Among all the leaders of the world, Jesus stands out as especially unique. He was unique in His birth, His teaching, His miracles, His death, and His resurrection. We all have seen the film about His life, but now we will read about Him out of the book of the Christian faith, the Bible.

"Today, I will give each of you a portion of the Bible called the New Testament. It is the part that tells the truth about what Jesus said and did. It is divided into books that were written by people who lived at the time of Jesus. Each book is divided into chapters, and each chapter is divided into verses. These verses have numbers by them so you can find very good quotes by Jesus very easily.

"Please turn to the book of St. Luke. You can find the page in the table of contents. Now turn to chapter two and we will read verses one through eleven about the uniqueness of the birth of Jesus." One of the young men near the front of the room signaled that he had found the passage. She called on him, and he stood by his desk and read the passage aloud.

"Now we need to know about the forgiveness of Jesus," she said, calling on one of the other students to read the story of the prodigal son. There was no coercion on her part, but her teaching on the uniqueness of Jesus was as fine as any I had ever heard. It was exactly right. And the students were extremely interested. I wondered how long this open door would last. I was thankful we had moved quickly.

As we walked from school to school, I got the overall report from Bob. The team in Vladimir had opened the ministry in 117 schools. More than 7,000 students and 1,000 teachers had seen the film. They had scores of teachers in discipleship groups and 42 schools were currently teaching the Christian Ethics and Morality course.

At School 10, CoMission staff member Joy Wease had explained to an English class for eight- and nine-year-olds why the Bible is a reliable help to answer the most important questions of life. They were studying bilingual New Testaments that Joy had provided for them. Four teachers from other schools had come to observe how the course could be included as part of the English curriculum.

The class had written essays in English on why the Bible is important. I got a copy of one:

> After the great October Revolution, some cathedrals and churches were destroyed. Communists made a big historical mistake. They betrayed God. But He forgave them. And I think that best thing in the world and in the life is to forgive other people. As for me, I think that Bible must be important for all people, because in first place, Bible made our culture rich. In the second place, Bible teaches us be kind, do good deeds, forgive other people.   —Alexi

It was pretty good insight, I thought, from students who were just beginning to understand that there was a solid basis on which to determine what was right and wrong—apart from the teachings of Marx and the Communist Party. I looked at a couple of others:

> I am fond of the Bible and I can say that it is very important for our life. In the Bible we learn a lot of rules. We read about the creation of the world. We know more about Jesus and His life. We read there: Don't steal, since that is atheism. Don't be mean to friends and other people. Don't say anything false, and don't go on wrong track. Always love and remember our God.
> —N. Stepanova

> The Bible is important. Why? Because in the Bible we read God's laws. God teaches us to be kind, good, and to love people. When I read the Bible, I think what good things I do on this day, week, month, year. And I want to do more good things.
> If all people will love God and if they read the Bible, killers will not kill and thieves will not steal. When all people love God, there will not be wars and it will be peace on the earth. There will be nice gardens, forests, and fields. There will be many flowers in the streets. Rivers, lakes, seas and oceans will be clear and

there will be fish in the water. People will be happy to see other people. And all people will treat animals and birds well. And will be good in the world when all people read the Bible and love God.   —Sasha

Was the "JESUS" film and the Christian ethics course making a difference in the lives of the next generation in Russia? I was thrilled.

During the remainder of the day, I visited teacher education classes and talked with principals and teachers in five schools. Several times I met teachers who were presenting the course but were not yet believers themselves.

They told me they felt that after being Communists for forty years, it was too late for them to change. But their students deserved that right to make a choice to follow Jesus if they wanted to. And they would give them that opportunity.

In a teachers' lounge in School 25, I met a teacher who had married a Muslim Tatar man. She had found Christ and had led her daughters and grandchildren to Christ. They all had been baptized a few weeks before.

"What made you decide to become a believer?" I asked.

Her answer was simple: "Bob and Sally."

"What do you mean?" I pressed.

"All of our lives," she explained, "we have heard propaganda. We decided that Christianity was just more propaganda. But when I saw the lives of Bob and Sally and how they showed the love of Jesus, I decided to believe."

At first, I wasn't sure about this answer. It seemed that she should believe because of the truth of the Bible. But just as quickly, I realized that in Russia the truth of God needs to be expressed in people. In fact, His plan indicates that each of us should reflect what God is like when others look at our lives. If we are filled with and controlled by His Holy Spirit, other people can see in our lives the kind of love, joy, peace, patience, and self-control that Jesus had. And they will be drawn to Him.

The teachers of Vladimir saw Jesus in the lives of Bob and Sally and they were drawn to Him. Above and beyond all the teaching that the CoMission teams were doing, they were living demonstrations of how a person looked and acted when he or she became a true believer in Jesus.

And I thought, *That's what Jesus wants for me and my family, and the people in my church—all of us.* He wants His presence in us to be so obvious in our love, in our actions, in our smiles, even in our pain, that people will be drawn to Him. While we are taking the gospel to the world, we need to live it in our own home towns.

As I returned from Russia, I reflected on the amazing events that had taken place during the past few years. From the premiere in Moscow to the classroom experience in Vladimir had been just 36 months. The premieres had been held in 35 cities, and 13 million copies of the Gospel of Luke had been distributed as the film showed in 2,000 theaters. Convocations had been held in 92 cities for 28,000 teachers. And the CoMission was sending hundreds of workers into the field.

Still, so many places had not yet heard the message. Thousands of unreached people groups still needed to be contacted. The same God who opened the Soviet bloc and tore down the Iron Curtain was still not willing that any should perish.

Billboards throughout the former Soviet Union announce the first Christian film ever to be shown publicly, ultimately in two thousand theaters.

The future is in the hands of our Lord. He is the one who rules in the affairs of men and nations. He is the one who has all authority in heaven and on earth. It is Jesus whom we lift up. And if He is lifted up, He Himself has said that He will draw all men unto Himself. This is the greatest promise in all the world.

In light of this promise, we believe that what we have seen is only a glimpse of what lies ahead. Now is the time to keep pushing out the borders and to keep pressing on to new frontiers.

CHAPTER 26

The Greatest Commission

I s it possible for everyone, everywhere, to hear the message of Christ? Is it possible to show the "JESUS" film to the whole world? Can it be done? My answer is, "Absolutely, positively, yes!"

Since the launch of the "JESUS" film in 1980, viewership exceeds five billion. With the growing world population, there are still so many who have never heard the name of Jesus. But, there is great hope.

A new, growing wave of men and women believe we really can take the message of Jesus to the whole world. At the start of the new century, a whole new wind of the Holy Spirit blows across our world.

A rapidly expanding cadre of committed believers from every denominational and confessional background once again calls the attention of the Church back to our Lord's final commission to us, given in Matthew 28:18–20:

> Then Jesus came to them and said, "All authority in heaven and on earth has been given to me. Therefore go and make disciples of all nations, baptizing them in the name of the Father and of the Son and of the Holy Spirit, and teaching them to obey everything I have commanded you. And surely I am with you always, to the very end of the age."

This passage of Scripture contains what has been called the "Great Commission" of our Lord. It is the greatest commission, the grandest assignment, ever given in the history of mankind. It is the only admonition in all of creation that, when it is followed, will result in people's lives being changed for all eternity.

This command has driven men and women throughout the centuries to leave the security and comfort of their own societies and go to the ends of the earth with the matchless message of the love and forgiveness of Jesus.

It is my prayer that the "JESUS" film will be one of the tools the Lord will use to accomplish His plan for everyone to hear the gospel. All I have recounted for you in these pages has been only a glimpse of what is happening—and in only a few areas of the vast harvest. It is also only a prelude to what I believe God will do in the future.

I have often said that I believe we are living in one of the most exciting times in all of human history. If I could choose any time to be alive, I would choose right now. I believe we are seeing the fulfillment of Matthew 24:14 where Jesus told his disciples, "This gospel of the kingdom will be preached in the whole world as a testimony to all nations, and then the end will come."

I believe we may be living in the generation that will see the gospel preached to the whole world. With all of my heart, I want to be a part of it.

Mike Milchling checks a newly produced soundtrack master. Behind him are the original 700 master language tracks.

The "JESUS" film belongs to the body of Christ. It is God's Word, and He has blessed it. We feel our responsibility is simply to make it as widely available as possible. To date, more than 1,500 different missions and denominations have used the film. We count it a privilege to be their servants, to help them get the film in the languages they need for the tribes and people groups they are attempting to reach.

The plans are simple, but extremely challenging. The first step is to complete the translation of the film into 1,800 languages. This is currently the number of languages in the world that are spoken by at least 50,000 people. These languages include 99 percent of the world's population. At this writing, we have completed more than 750 translations and another 236 are in various stages of development. To complete the task will require many more engineers, administrators, support staff, and a $35,000 budget for each translation.

The distribution plan calls for a variety of approaches depending on the media sophistication of the country or area. They range from theatrical releases, television showings, and cable TV releases by satellite to 16mm films that teams take into the deepest jungle by canoe.

The "JESUS" film will be available in video rental shops in a variety of languages, and will be distributed to homes, schools, hospitals, and libraries by methods we are not even aware of yet.

We will need 77 different sign languages to reach 400 million deaf and hearing-impaired people. A dramatic audio/radio version will be distributed to 42 million people who are blind, as well as those living in places where little access exists for the film.

Our ministry will need to launch more than 3,000 film teams, and many others will need to be started by other organizations. They will require thousands of sets of equipment, film prints, and follow-up literature. At the time of this writing, more than 2,800 teams are already in the field, and more than 12,000 16mm copies of the film and more than 35 million videocassettes, VCDs (video compact discs), and DVDs (digital video discs) are in circulation.

At least a thousand New Life Training Centers need to be launched. These centers would provide leaders for all the New Life groups being formed to follow up the showings, and also pastors for the thousands of new churches being planted.

To back up and support all these activities, three great essentials exist: prayer, people, and finances.

Hundreds of people are needed in support roles—administrators, secretaries, teachers, accountants, engineers, and a host of others. Millions of dollars must be raised, and thousands of people must pray.

Our responsibility in all of this is simply to be available, and willing, and yielded to do whatever He wants us to do with our lives. We must see a world that desperately needs to feel the touch of Jesus.

I will never forget a particular moment in a field in the Karamoja region of northern Uganda. It was, for me, a great moment of truth and conviction.

When our plane landed on a grassy air strip, we were greeted by native tribesmen armed with spears. Because of tribal warfare in the area, all the cattle belonging to the Karamoja had been stolen, and 185,000 people had died of starvation within just a few months.

They took us to a field where we saw a pile of skulls, maybe six feet high. I picked up two of the skulls, one in each hand, and held them. As I looked at them, I realized that six months earlier these were people who had been alive. They had been living, breathing human beings who had simply starved to death.

I held their skulls and wondered if they had ever had one opportunity to hear the message of Christ. I wondered how much people in this region knew about who Jesus really was.

That afternoon we entered a little village, and I asked my interpreter to help us find out what people knew about Jesus. We lined up fourteen or fifteen individuals, and I began to ask them one at a time, "Tell me, what do you know about Jesus?"

One by one they shook their heads and said, "I don't know Him." "Where does He live?" "No, I never heard of Him." We came to the last person, a little eight-year-old boy. I said to the interpreter, "Just ask him to tell me anything, anything at all, that he's ever heard about Jesus."

A big tear ran down the little boy's face, and the interpreter said, "Sir, he would like to tell you about Jesus, but he has never before heard the name."

It's not fair, I thought, *that there should be so many opportunities to receive Christ in our country, and this small child doesn't get one chance to hear the message.*

I realized that day that I am only one person—but whatever I can do, I want to make sure that there are no little boys or girls, or men or women, who don't get that one opportunity, that one chance to hear about Jesus and who He is. Everyone, everywhere, needs and deserves to feel His wonderful, tender, loving, merciful, healing, protecting, empowering, and oh-so-forgiving touch.

This is a divine moment in history for the body of Christ to unite in one great thrust for the kingdom. After having this Good News for two thousand years, it is time to make sure that, as much as it lies within our power, we have done everything we know to get the message of Jesus to every person in the world.

This story is not finished. It has just begun. These accounts of people coming into the kingdom are just a small glimpse of what our wonderful Lord is doing. All praise and glory and honor go to Him! We look forward to that day when every knee in heaven and on earth will bow before our powerful Savior. Until that day, perhaps He will continue to use this film to help fulfill the greatest commission of all time, to help bring many more spiritually hungry people into His kingdom. In every country of the world, may those who have been struggling to find peace with God feel *the touch of Jesus.*